FUTURE
WHAT NEEDS
TO DEVELOP

JOHN LOK

Copyright © John Lok
All Rights Reserved.

Contents

PREFACE

Introduction
What are the different unique characteristics between one developing country and one developed country ? How to judge whether the country had been either developed or had been developing ? What factors influence the country development speed? In my this book, I shall indicate New Zealand whether is one developed country or developing country, although its farming industry , e.g. sheep cloth manufacturing, breef and pork meat food export industries had developed long time, but what weaknesses, it owns to influence its continue development easily as well as what strengths it lacks to influence New Zealand is still staying in the developing stage in possible in global leading position. What factors influence US, UK their technological development can not be continued innovated to cause worse development to compare Germany 's heavy manufacturing industry future development in possible.

In our societies, how developing and developed countries can apply robotics to improve themselves countries social development to be better, even the best. Can robotic development be applied to help developed and developing noth to improve their societies in success? Can robotic development only be applied to help developed countries to improve their societies more easier to compare developing countries? Is it difficult or it is not possible to apply robotic development to any developing countries?

In my this book, I shall let readers to attempt to make judgement whether AI can improve manufacturing efficiency, marketing development, creating jobs, changing public transport to none manual driving public tranport tools and space technological development to assist only developed countries.

• viii •

PROLOGUE

● Global resource is shortage to allocate unfair
challenge p.66-70
● Some developed countries have obligation to help
developing countries
● Rich countries have responsibilites to assist global
economy development or balance economy development
    Methods developing countries can
become developed countries
● Main industries aspects need to develop p.71-80
● The challenges are needed to solve in development
process
● What a developing country should do to be a developed
one?
● Developed Countries need to help Developing Countries
to increase their competitive effort in societies
Can bring global benefit when all
countries are developed countries
1. How Globalization Affects Developed
Countries
Conflicting Globalization Views
● Benefits of globalization
● Drawbacks of globalization
● What Is Globalization?
● Why and how globalization may achieve
when global countries can develop
to become developed countries ?
● Components of Globalization
● The degree to which an organization is globalized and
diversified has bearing on the strategies that it uses to
pursue greater development and investment opportunities.
● Effect of globalization on developing countries or third
world countries

● What influences to the countries like china and India has grown tremendously after globalization.

● Effect of globalization on developed countries when all developing countries can become developed countries

● Development of "Regional economic" will truly help India to build viable economic future for its citizens.

● Regional economies help to reduce domination of developed economies on the developing economies.

　2. Economic growth advantages and disadvantages

● Are economic growth and development worthwhile?

● Economic growth and development of Asia when all or many developing countries can develop to be developed countries

● Model of economy development: The production function how can be influenced to change when many or all developing countries can become developed countries

● How global developed economy influences household expenditure decision?

● How global developed economy influences the labor supply function changes ?

● How global developed economy influences wage rate versus labor leisure changes?

● Economic development theories: Harrod-Domar theory
　　Will developed countries become
developing countries

● Why does illness can cause global economic recession to developed countries p.81-91

● Increasing social crime rate and government assistance may cause developed countries to become developing coutries

● Developed countries lack effort to manufacture cheap products to sell strengths

● Climate change will impact developed countries to continue develop

1.1 Positive social change influence to vehicle fuel consumers

1.2 Negative social change influence

1.3 Terrorisms attack influence

● Can airline fuel self-organization avoid fuel price rising cost

● Can tourism industry influence airline profitability

● Is fuel price rising only factor to cause airline risk in short term

● Methods to solve rising air fare prices to decrease travellers'demand

Biofuels energy increases supply

Reducing terrorism occurrence

● Will airline industry's ticket price elasticity be influenced by demand and supply factor

● Boeing 747 manufacturing fuel cost strategy

● How airlines and airports implement successful netwpork strategies

● Performance measurement system strategy

● What factors influence cost-related management quality ?

● Economic Environment Influences Airport
service performance

Economic Environment Influences Airport
service performance

Airline employee positive emotion method
    Emotional labor factor

I

Defining developed and developing countries differences

● What are the developed countries and developing countries
characteristics
What factors cause the differences between developed countries and developing countries? Do they have significant unique characteristics to be discovered to influence their differences? I shall attempt to indicate evidences to explain whether these are significant different unique characteristics between any developed countries and developed countries as below:
ON economic measurement aspect, low-and middle income economies are usually referred to as developing economies

, and the upper middle income and the high income are referred to as developed countries. So, a developing country also called a less developed country or emerging market, it has a lower gross domestic product(GDP) than developed countries, with a less nature and sophisticated economy. The difference is between developed and developing countries. It may indicate that developed countries refer to the Sovereign (independent) nation/state whose economy has highly progressed and possesses great technological improvement, as compared to other nations.

The countries with low industrialization and low human development indix are formed as developing countries. The World Bank classified the world's economies into four groups, based on Gross National Income per capita: high, upper middle, lower-middle , and low income countries. Least developed countries, landlocked developing countries and small island developing states are all sub-groupings of developing countries. However, it is not ensure that it is only all islands are developing countries, e.g. New Zealand may be one developing country or low developed country also. Experts have said the Guyana has one of the fastest -growing economies in the world.

The unique characteristics differences between developed countries and developing countries. They may include: developing countries are ususally poor, according to the Asian development bank, the major causes of poverty may include: Low economic growth, a week agricultural sector, increased population rates and a high volume of inequality. So, the features of developing countries, their common characteristics may include: low per capita real income, low per capita real income is one of the most defining because amony any developed countries , they may also include highly and lowly developed countries. For example, Norway is the most developed nation in the world. Switzerland is the second developed country in the world, Ireland is the third-most developed country. Then all of these nations may be highly developed countries , e.g. Germany, Hong Kong, China, Australia, Iceland, Sweden. So , it seems that New Zealand may be a lowly developed country to compare above these highly developed countries.

● What factors assist the developing countries to become developed countries

However, the most developing countries in the world, they may include India, Brazil, China, Argentina is actually considered a developing country and characteristics of developing economies, high population is continue growing. Otherwise, China had began to use methods to discourage Chinese families to born more than one child in order to avoid population continue grows to bring social future burden.

Dependence on primary sector, e.g. Africa and India and New Zealand , they were still depending on main agricutural fruit, rice primary farming industry for themselves main GDP export income source as well as dependence on exports of primary commodities. So, developing countries should need focus on human development, it will remain the main focus of developing countriespost 2015 year. In this regard, the transition of developed countries to equitable and sustainable consumption will make in easier for developinf countries to pursue their human development goals in a more environmental susttainable way.

Hence, human development will may to help developing countries to develop more easily. It is future essential element to assist any one developing countries to be developed countries in success.

The unique characteristics of developing countries include that: Literacy rate is quite low as people are deprived of education facilities, the standard of living in developing countries is normally not very high. Otherwise, developed countries literacy rate is quite high , due to better education ayatem and life expectancy rate is more , due to better standing living. So, in general, the standard of living is very high to developed countries, e.g. UK, US , they have many the low income level or poor people still may have enough money to save in bank and the number of poor people is less in themselves countries, due to definitional discrepancies countries, such as Maxico, Greece and Turkey. India may be nowadays developing countries.

However, there are agrument or disagreement between developed and developing countries. The developed countries say that developing countries must stop burning fossil, fuels and other things that harm the atmosphere. Otherwise, developing countries argue that developed countries have developed by burning the fossil fuels. They say their development will be affected if they stop burning fuels. For Japan example, it is one highly developed country because ir is one of the largest and most developed economies in the world. It has a well-educated, industrious workforce and its large , affluent population makes it is one of the world's biggest consumer markets. Otherwisem New Zealand is not high technological and industrious developed country, it still depends on agricultural fruits, meats export farming industry for main GDP growth source. So, comparison New Zealand and Japan development speed, New Zealand is one lowly developed country. Otherwise, Japan is one highly developed country in nowadays our society. But, the comparison between New Zealand and China, China is still a developing country , but New Zealand may be one lowly developed country to compare China because Chinese government has repeatedly stated that China is the world's largest developing country, despite rapid economic growth over the past four decades. However, according to the 2018 survey, the United States is the world's most powerful country, following countries may include: Japan, Israel, South Korea, Saudi, Arabia, but the safest country may be Iceland because its crime rate is the least. Although, US, UK may be highly developed countries, but their crime rate may be high position. So, one highly developed country does not represent that it must have the most safest social living environment to let its citizen to feel safe to live. It may be any one highly developed countries themselves failure points.

However, environmental factors may also stop a country from developing because some places experience environmental issues, which can present them from developing, examples might be extremee flooding or desertification social factors may also stop a country from developing, e.g. high crime rate, high unemployed rate, low safe living feeling rate, low living standard, they are some parts of the world have issues that are caused by people to influence any countries continue to develop to be one developed country easily. So, all of these factors can assist any one developing country to become developed country.

II

What factors cause developed countries continue developed

What factors cause New Zealand to be developed country in success

What factors influence New Zealand is still one lowly developed country? Can New Zealand fight itself country weaknesses to become one highly developed country? I shall attempt to indicate several evidences to explain what factors influence New Zealand can not develop to reach mature social development stage in itself nowadays society are below:

New Zealand is a small population country. It has only 4.8 million . However, there are many NZ people feel poverty to live. The causes of poverty in New Zealand. They may include: income inequality, lack of a simple fund support from government, lack of economic infrastructure, poor access to education, poor access to healthcase, opinion was evenly diviced on the primary cause of child poverty in NZ. Forty percent of NZ people said it was due to economic factors including unemployment, low wages, and rising living costs, the ever-increasing monthly power bills the the NZ government won't regulate or gone down.

However, in NZ, poverty is seen as relative, whereby those suffering deprivation are often struggling to feed their children, living in insecurce circumstances and unable to enjoy a satisfying social life easily to many New Zealanders. As a result, many NZ family members' health suffers and children fail to achieve a sound level of education. IN fact, there is poverty in the midst of prosperity in NZ. There is poverty amidst prosperity: There are around 682,500 people in poverty in this country or one in seven households, including around 220, 000 children .

In general, there are the causes of poverty reasons to any countries, they may include: lack of good jobs / job growth, lack of good education, the second root causes of poverty is a lack of education, a lack of social welfare, weather/climate change, social injustice, lack of food and water, lack of government support. Although NZ may be belonged to one developed country. But, it is still staying on the lowly developed stage in long time development process. The main factors cause NZ is still one lowly developed country. They may include : lack of good jobs growth in order to let graduates can find good jobs to do and education level can not be improved . What factors cause NZ lacks good job growht and poor education improvement in long time?

In fact, NZ likes many developed countries, its witnessing a transformation in itself economy and employment opportunities. Its traditional exporting sectors , such as dairy, meat, forestry and tourism, remain important drivers of growth. So, NZ's main source of income, they are agricutlural products export, principally meat, dairy products, and fruits and vegetables , crude oil and wood and paper products are also significant. However, the impacts of poverty in NZ, because children in poor communities are three times more likely than the average child to be sick twice as likely to end up in hospital, and sudden unexpected death in infancy rates are more than 6 times higher for infants in the most disadvantaged areas of NZ. These harmful effects run into adulthood in NZ.

What are the most common jobs in NZ? The most popular carre was police officer. SO, when many NZ people hope to seek policeforce jobs. NZ will bring poor job growth development chance to let graduates have plans to develop other professional career in society. Many NZ graduates only consider policeforce jobs, it is one poor social job culture in NZ. However, NZ education is better than America in possible. NZ is definitely superior to the US, in the OECD nations indication, NZ is ranked 3 rd for education quality behinf Finland and Canada, the US ranks about 12 th . Why does NZ still be one lowly developed country in possible, when it can have superior education system?

In fact, NZ ranks highly on most indicators of well-being, but average social level of incomes are low , in general, inequality income were allocated and made NZ economy less developed in the face of shocks, due to low labour productivity factor, low labour productiviey is only partly explained by the farming main industry of the NZ economy and is primarily a consequence of low mulit-factor productivity growth within NZ other industries development, instead of farming industry as well as weak investment on other industries, e.g. technololgical, computer manufacturing , medicine life science drug manufacturing, construction, engineering, e.g. robotic manufacturing etc. different industries development. So, NZ neglects to consider how to develop other industries instead of concentrating on only development on agricultural industry.

However, economic geography is an important factor in NZ's poor productivity performance as the small size and remoteness of the economy diminish its access to global markets, the scale and efficiency of domestic businesses, the level of competition, and the ability to benefit from innovation at the global frontier. All of these many be the main cause weaknesses to NZ countinue development in success.

Moreover, NZ government lacks good policy to support its productivity growth, e.g. lacking to promoting international connections, none removing barriers to fixed capital investment to NZ domestic any industries development, instead of agricultural industry, accessing benefits of agricultural industry, accessingg benefits by improving urban planninf, enhancing competition and increasing investment in innovation and intangibles.

Hence, poor productivity technological improvement may be on main factor to cause NZ productivity growth is poor. It is main reason to cause NZ is one lowly developed country in long time, because global highly developed countries concerned high technological productivity is expected to be the main driver of income source , in particular via investment in technology and knowledge-based capital. So, any highly developed countries began to believe that economic growth from productivity improvements contributes to welfare through increasing the worker individual income that can be earned from each hour worked, providing individuals with the option to work lesss or consume moew job and service. Hence , NZ lacks high technological productivity improved to let any one talent NZ person can have chance to use his / her talent knowledge to do high technological jobs in order to attribute NZ society and to earn high hour income. NZ is only developing agricultural industry nowadays. SO, agricultural jobs wil be common jobs in NZ developed country. Hence, low technolgical productive improvement may be main factor to influence NZ to be one lowly developed country in long time.

What factors influence US and UK continue development
Why do US and US be a developed country? It has a high-income economy and a very high human development index rating. Ranking 13 th in the world. Today, the UK , US remains one of the world's great powers with considerable economc, cultural , military, scientific, technological and political influence internationally. Why are UK and US econome so strong? It's quality of life is generally considered high, and the economy is quite diversified . The sectors that contibute must be the US, UK 's GDP are services, manufacturing, construction and tourism . Moreover, UK and US are the world's largest economy by normimal GDP and net wealth and they are the second largest by purchasing power. Themselves nations's economy is fueled by natural resources, a well-developed and high productivity.
It seems that UK and US have a mixed economic development, developed through free market and global economy , which are regulated by their governments to prevent market failure easily.

III

What Factors Influence Social Development Speed

What factors cause why some countries can develop rapidly ? What factors cause some countries develop slowly? It would be hard to find a more fundamental conept for the social development and human development. The social development science is about human societies how we develop, so we had better have some idea to explain how and why what factors cause some countries can develop rapidly , e.g. US, UK, or what factors cause some countries can develop slowly, e.g. China, India. The reaons that there has been a question about the development speed to any countries , it has been an active and influential movement to insist that this was a human social development question. Why does Inida has many years history, otherwise, US has less many years histroy, what factors influence US can develop more rapidly to compare Inida? Even, India seems to be one developing country in nowadays society.

From sociobiology to social development psychology

What factors to India is facing to influence it can not succeed to develop to be highly developed country easily? Human cognitive mechanisms evolved in the Pleistocene, the period from about 2 million years ago, about 10,000 years ago, the end of the last Ice age, MOtivating this choice is the thought that substantial periods of development time are required for significant evoluntionary change, such as social need change, family need change, country need change. Much of Evolutinnary psychology has consisted of reflection on the different countries changing conditions that might have obtained during this perios, and the human development behaviors what would have been most favoured by natural selection given those conditions.

First of all to what influences human feels we need to develop, a lot of human behavior has roots that are far more ancient. Sociability , for instance, is not a uniquely human attribute. But significant changes in the nature of human sociality are evident over historical periods of tens or hundrends of years, presumably because they are due to cultural improvement, or raising human cultural quality , so our cultural improvement psychology influences why some countries can not develop rapidly, such as India does not consider itself Indian cultural level needs to raise significantly. Otherwise, US condiers itself American cultural level need to raise significantly. So, this cultural development reason may explain why India is still one developing country, although, its has many years history to compare US.

Social Development Psychology
Another important point about social development issus, it is the environmental factor, it is one picture to influence why some countries develop rapidly , but some countries still develop slowly. I don nor need to pursue that argument , since the focus will remain on the human development case, and no one could suppose that the social enviroment that human create for, among the other things, the production of new human social behaviors, is simply a consequence of genetically determined human behavior. For example, American hopes that it can create many talent people to help itself country to develop, so talent people development environment need can influence US can have many talent people to create to help itself country to develop to be highly developed country in short time, e..g. space science, life science etc.

I wished to emphasize particularly the ability of cultural evolution to transform the social development history to different countries issus. It seems clear that humans have learned in quite recent time to construct a remarkably social changing environment for the development for their young. So, any countries their future development, they must depend on how many talent young people, they can create. It is very important issue to influence any one country to develop to be one high developed or low developed or developing country. For that reason their introduction should be seen as representing major cultural improvemernt and social environment factors to influence any countries their future development speed. For this simple example, many further illustrate the point, they indicate that the mobile phone did not exist when I was a child. In fact, it is for hardly more than a decade that it has been for everyday life in developed countries. Ans whereas it may seem only more or less need for people of my generation, for those aged, say 10 to 20 , age, it is as unthinkable to deprived of one's phone as to wander the streets stark naked. Most teenagers move through the would, when this smart phone technological development, it can influence any one feels that it is essential product to our daily need. It is one cultural improvement factor example , it can explain why global many people feel smart phones are essential product to satisfy us need. It is not, therefore, merely behavior that has changed for those who have grown up with the mobile phone, but the social environment can bring indirect to influence any one , even old age feels smart phone need, when old age people can contact many young people , they must own least one smart phone for personal use. So, cultural improvement and social environment changing need both factors can influence any one country may make development decision in short time or long time, when the country people feel that they have urgent social and cultural improvement changing need rapidly.

IV

What are the differences between developing and developed countries

I shall explain the difference between developed and developing countries characteristics as below:

Countries are divided into two major categories by the United Nations, which are developed countries and developing countries. The classification of countries is based on the economic status such as GDP, GNP, per capita income, industrialization, the standard of living, etc.

Developed Countries refers to the soverign state, whose economy has highly progressed and possesses great technological infrastructure, as compared to other nations. The countries with low industrialization and low human development index are termed as developing countries. Developed Countries provides free, healthy and secured atmosphere to live whereas developing countries, lacks these things.

The characteristics between developing and developed countries may include as below:

Developed countries means that a country having an effective rate of industrialization and individual income is known as Developed Country. Otherwise, developing Country is a country which has a slow rate of industrialization and low per capita income. Developed countries have low unemployment and poverty, developing countries have usually high unemployment and poverty. developed countries have low infant mortality rate, death rate and birth rate is low while the life expectancy rate is high. Otherwise, developing countries have high infant mortality rate, death rate and birth rate, along with low life expectancy rate. Developed countries have better living conditions and high standard of living, but developing countries have bad living conditions and low standard of living. Developing countries have high GDP from industrial sector income source, otherwise, developed countries have high GDP income from service sector income source. Developing countries have high industrial growth. Otherwise, developed countries, they rely on the developed countries for their growth. Developed countries have high equal of distribution of income, otherwise, developing countries have high unequal of distribution of income. Finally, developed countries have effectively utilized to factors of production, otherwise, developing countries have ineffectively utilized to factors of production. Overall , any thing of developed countries are better than developing countries in nowadays societies.

Between developed and developing countries, one can identify a variety of differences. This differentiation of countries, as developed and developing, is used to classify countries according to their economic status based on per capita income, industrialization, literacy rate, living standards, etc.

● What are Developed Countries?

They have usually these similar characteristics as below:

(1) Developed countries have industrial growth and enjoy flourishing economy. Developed countries experience marked development and growth in the areas such as transportation, business, and education. Developed countries are characterized by a low death rate and low birth rate as well. There is usually a very small gap between the two rates in developed countries.

(2) Developed countries are not characterized by shortcomings. They are well-developed in all fronts and are served well by water supplies, amenities, educational institutions, health care concerns. This is because of the fact that people are endowed with awareness about every possible aspect relating to human existence. The absence of shortcomings in the developed countries is possibly due to the fact there is a low birth rate in these countries. Nutrition is available in plenty to mothers and infants in developed countries.

● What are Developing Countries?

They have usually these similar characteristics as below:

(1) Developing countries depend on the developed countries for help to establish their industries. They have only begun

to taste the growth of the economy. Developing countries are in the beginning stages of development in the areas of education, business, and transportation.

(2) Developing countries are characterized by many shortcomings. These shortcomings include less awareness regarding matters relating to health, poor amenities, shortage in water supply, shortcoming in the area of medical supply, a higher rate of birth rate. The most important and worrying factor in the developing countries is the factor of poor nutrition. Poor nutrition to both mothers and infants is the main concern in the developing countries. Due to high birth rates, the probability of natural diseases is more in developing countries. Hence, the death rates are also eventually high in developing countries. However, since natural diseases increase by high rates in the developing countries, they will have a short population doubling time. In the case of developing countries, there is usually a big gap between the birth rate and the death rate. Infant mortality factor is influenced by the development factor of countries. A developing country for that matter would have higher infant mortality than a developed country.

Overall, economists will differ their different characteristcs from these several aspects as below:

Developed countries display a high level of development. Developing countries: Developing countries display a lower development in different areas such as industrialization, human capital, etc. Developed countries have industrial growth. Developing countries depend on the developed countries for help to establish their industries. Developed countries enjoy flourishing economy. Developing countries begin to taste the growth of the economy. Developed countries experience marked development and growth in the areas such as transportation, business, and education. Developing countries are in the beginning stages of development in the areas of education, business, and transportation. Developed countries are characterized by a low death rate and low birth rate as well. There is usually a very small gap between the two rates in developed countries. In developing countries there is usually a big gap between the birth rate and the death rate. Hence, in overall, any aspects are worse, slow growth to developing countries compare to developed countries.

● What are general their GDP difference

Developed Countries:

A developed nation is one that has a very high rank in industrial advancement, constructs its economy in light of innovation and assembling rather than agribusiness. The variables of production, for example, human and regular assets are completely used bringing about an increment underway and utilization which prompts a very high rank in per capita salary. A nation with a more Human Development Index (HDI) is viewed as a developed nation. It not just measures the financial improvement and GDP of a nation additionally its instruction and future.

Developing Countries:

A developing nation is those having a way of life or level of modern advancements well beneath that conceivable with money related or specialized guide; a nation that is not yet exceptionally industrialized. A country having less utilization of resources and low income per capita which leads to low GDP of a country.

● Developed VS Developing Countries will have different development or growth speed to compare as below:

?Industrial Economies:

In developed countries, economy depends on industrial sector instead of agriculture sector. There is more development in industrial sector. In developing countries, mostly economy depends on agriculture sector and they are moving toward industrialization.

?Citizens:

In developed countries, citizens and well off and rich. In developing countries, proportion of rich citizens is very low.

?Unemployment:

In developed countries, there is no such issue of unemployment. They provide many employment opportunities to the citizens. In developing countries, issue of unemployment is there and it affects the economy of country very badly.

?Education:

The growth rate in education sector is very high in developed countries and they have best education systems. Whereas the growth rate of developing countries in education sector is low as compare to developed countries. While developing countries are following the education system of developed countries to achieve the standard.

?Technological advantages:

In developed countries, every place is full with technological advancements and they always try to make it better. In developing countries, there are many undeveloped rural areas and even urban sector have less technological advancements.

?Roads:

Developed countries have a very sound infrastructure by having better roads, railway tracks, airports etc. Developing countries don't have a sound infrastructure as compare to developed countries.

?Government:

There exists stable government in developed countries so that they make effective and reliable policies for better economic development. Developing countries have unstable governments and mostly try to following the policies made by developed countries.

?Health care:

In developed countries, good and better facilities for health have been provided to citizens. In developing countries, health care facilities are not so good and acceptable.

?Resources:

In developed countries, the natural and human resources are fully and efficiently consumed. In developing countries, many of the natural resources are still untouched and others resources are also not fully utilized.

?Income:

There is a high level of income as per citizen living in developed country so that they have high GDP and GNP. Developing countries have low level of income as per citizen living in country with unequal distribution of income as that have low GDP and GNP.

?High Human Development Index (HDI):

In developed countries, there are best education systems and better health care and high income level so this leads to high value and ranking of HDI. In developing countries, there are low income level and fewer facilities for health care and low rates of education so this leads to low or middle ranking in HDI.

?Life expectancy:

In developed countries, due to better health care the life expectancy has been increased and they have low birth rates as well as low death rates. In developing countries, life expectancy is not so high but has high rates of birth and death due to less facilities and education.

?Water and food supply:

In developed countries, safe and clean water is supplied with plentiful supply of food items and good housing condition. In developing countries, dirty and unsafe water is supplied with less reliable food items and poor condition of houses.

In conclusion, all our daily necessary need and social need to developing countries growth will be worse to compare developed countries in our nowadays societies.

● How to measure the difference between developed and developing countries ?

The measurement factors between developed and developing countries may include as below:

(1) GDP factor

The classification of a country does not only depend on its income but also on other factors that affect how their citizens live, how their economies are integrated into the global system, and the expansion and diversification of their export industries. A developed country is one that has a high level of industrial development, bases its economy on technology and manufacturing instead of agriculture. The factors of production such as human and natural resources are fully utilized resulting in an increase in production and consumption which leads to a high level of per capita income. A country with a high Human Development Index (HDI) rating is considered a developed country. It not only measures the economic development and GDP of a country but also its education and life expectancy. A developed country's citizens enjoy a free and healthy existence.

(2) Industralization or Commercial aspect factor

The term "developed country" is synonymous to "industrialized country, post-industrial country, more developed country, advanced country, and first-world country." The United Kingdom, France, Germany, Canada, Japan, Switzerland, and the United States of America are only a few of those considered as developed countries. A developing country, on the other hand, is one that has a low level of industrialization.

It has a higher level of birth and death rates than developed countries. Its infant mortality rate is also high due to poor nutrition, shortage of medical services, and little knowledge on health. The citizens of developing countries have a low to medium standard of living because their per capita income is still developing, and their technological capacity is still being developed. There is also an unequal distribution of income in developing countries, and their factors of production are not fully utilized. Developing countries are also referred to as third-world countries or least-developed countries.

Countries are categorized according to their economic development. The United Nations classifies countries as developed, developing, newly industrialized or developed, and countries in transition such as Kazakhstan, Kyrgyztan, Turkmenistan, and the former USSR. The World Bank classifies countries according to their GNI per capita income: low income ($995 or less) and lower middle income ($996-$3,945); as developing countries with an upper middle income ($3,946-$12,195); and high income (above $11,906) as developed countries.

(3) The country citizen living of standard level

The classification of a country does not only depend on its income but also on other factors that affect how their citizens live, how their economies are integrated into the global system, and the expansion and diversification of their export industries. A developed country is one that has a high level of industrial development, bases its economy on technology and manufacturing instead of agriculture. The factors of production such as human and natural resources are fully utilized resulting in an increase in production and consumption which leads to a high level of per capita income. A country with a high Human Development Index (HDI) rating is considered a developed country. It not only measures the economic development and GDP of a country but also its education and life expectancy. A developed country's citizens enjoy a free and healthy existence.

The term "developed country" is synonymous to "industrialized country, post-industrial country, more developed country, advanced country, and first-world country." The United Kingdom, France, Germany, Canada, Japan, Switzerland, and the United States of America are only a few of those considered as developed countries.

A developing country, on the other hand, is one that has a low level of industrialization. It has a higher level of birth and death rates than developed countries. Its infant mortality rate is also high due to poor nutrition, shortage of medical services, and little knowledge on health. The citizens of developing countries have a low to medium standard of living because their per capita income is still developing, and their technological capacity is still being developed. There is also an unequal distribution of income in developing countries, and their factors of production are not fully utilized. Developing countries are also referred to as third-world countries or least-developed countries.

In conclusion, the measurement factors to decide whether the country is either developing or developed country. The factors depend on whether: whether the developed country is a country that has a high level of industrialization and per capita income while a developing country is a country that is still in the early stages of industrial development and has a low per capita income , whether the citizens of a developed country enjoy a free, healthy, and affluent existence while citizens of developing countries do not, whether the developed countries are also known as industrialized, advanced, and first-world countries while developing countries are also known as underdeveloped, least developed, and third-world countries. For example, The United States of America, Canada, Switzerland, Belgium, and France are examples of developed countries while India, Malawi, Honduras, the Philippines, and Rwanda are examples of developing countries as well as the infant mortality, birth, and death rates of developing countries are also higher compared to that of developed countries.

Why and how developed countries need
assist developing countries to develop

I think that we should help developing nations, But only to an extent. If we keep, And keep on giving them needs they will start to rely on foreign aid. I think charities are enough, But if the developing countries really need help then we give them help. But not too much, Basically they need to do something themselves and stop relying and take their own action. In exchange for our help maybe they could give us a bit of natural resources? Developing countries may need to be assisted, They may include these reasons:

● Global resource is shortage to allocate unfair challenge
Nowadays, global resources are not equally distributed in different countries. Thus, there are those who belong to the developed nations while there are others that belong to developing countries. With these unequal distribution, it is significant that developed countries must do their part in helping those who belong to the underprivileged sector. It is

true that rich countries have their own problems to worry with; Can we introduce aquaponics in developing countries when they don't have the resources that first world countries have? In many areas, there is no electricity available that is needed for many aquaponics systems; developing countries require simplicity, reliability, and freedom from the need of grid powerhowever, it is still their responsibility to help the developing countries people need to solve resource can not be allocated fair problem, such as Afria is one developing country, many people are drinking drink water, due to drought , so they will not feel health and they will feel sick , even die. It is one example of natural resource of clean water shortage challenge to Afica. So, developed country, e.g. US , it has responsibilty to help African to drink clean water because clean water is allocated to supply to America people to drink in preference, due to global clean water supply is decreasing, but human number is increasing and clean water demand will also increase. If clean water is only supplied to US people to drink , even other developed countries people , they can drink the most clean water. The reason is because Africa people is poor or dirty or low education level or it is one developing country etc. factors to influence many African can not often drink any clean water. It is very unfair to this developing country.

In 2010, there were 925 million hungry people in the world; 19 million in developed countries, 37 million in Near East and North Africa, 53 million in Latin America and the Caribbean, 239 Million in Sub-Saharan Africa, and 578 million in Asia and the Pacific. This means that approximately 1 in 7 people are hungry. Protein- energy malnutrition is the most lethal form of malnutrition/ hunger. It is a lack of calories and protein; protein is necessary for key bodily functions including provision of essential amino acids and the development and maintenance of muscles. Bringing aquaponics into third world countries would help prevent this problem by providing fish as a main source of protein. Poor nutrition is the cause or partial cause for at least half of the 10.9 million child deaths each year.

The number of hungry people has increased since 1997 due to three main problems: 1) neglect of agriculture relevant to very poor people by governments and international agencies; 2) worldwide economic crisis and 3) increase in food prices. Children who are poorly nourished suffer up to 160 days of illness each year. Malnutrition affects about 32% of children in developing countries. More than 70% of malnourished children live in Asia. Undernourished pregnant women in developing countries leads to 1 out of 6 infants born with low birth weight; this means higher neonatal death rates, increased occurrences of learning disabilities, mental retardation, poor health, blindness, and premature death. There is enough food to provide everyone in the world with 2, 720 kilocalories per person per day, however many people don't have the land to grow or the money to buy the food they need for themselves and their children. 1 out of 3 people in developing countries are affected by vitamin and mineral deficiency.

So, I feel that aid has diverse results. It can both harm as well help development. Rich countries might be sidetracked in terms of focusing on programs that will spur development. Asian and African nations should create long-term plans that will reduce the dependency on aid, while rich countries should transition from traditional methods of giving support in new ways. Rich countries still argue on the premise that they cannot afford aid or that they are being over-generous. The main idea here is not that they are questioning the aid itself, but the development project. Rich countries must be on the poor countries aid as these people from poor nations face injustice and hardships that are often caused or increased by the programs and decision of rich nations themselves.

However, giving aid is not really an act of generosity. Aid purchases things that donors desire. These might include political support in exchange for the "goodies" that the donor has provided. Rich countries must show support to the poor by abiding on the social, environmental aspects. It can also include adapting to climate change by changing one's own consumption. Another is to accept fairer trade rules. Moreover, rich countries can show true generosity by undergoing changes in the manner of living for the past few decades. It would be fair that rich countries believe they are being generous when they give out dole outs or loose change when poor people around the globe are trying to live on a few basics while living under the system that rich countries have developed. It is a reality that there are also poor people in rich countries that are undergoing tough times. However, it is not ethical to withdraw support from people abroad who are more underprivileged just because there are poor people in rich countries that need help as well.

In fact, many argue that the poor countries that rich countries provide financial aid are doing better economically. It is possible that these countries are growing and catching up with the standard of living. Say for example, the annual income of India might have greatly improved. However, when one divides that with the whole population, each Indian just obtains $3 or less per day. This issue requires obtaining the correct facts not only on financial aid, but on the act of generosity in this world. Rich countries do have a responsibility of giving to those developing country people's living need because they can enjoy any benefits in preference when resource is shortage and global need is also increasing in nowadays societies.

● Some developed countries have obligation to help developing countries

The rich have an obligation to help poor countries who were exploited by their colonial rulers. The United States had a head start with its vast natural resources. But many countries in Europe, such as Britain, became rich due to their colonial reign in Asia. They expanded their empire to include poor, resource-rich nations in Asia. They exploited the region's cheap labour, with workers getting little in return for their hard work. For Hong Kong , developing country and UK developed country. UK had obligation to help this developing country, HK before 1997.

Hong Kong was different though. Britain ruled Hong Kong for more than 150 years and I think both sides benefited. Today, the city is an international financial centre with a strong economy. But some countries did not benefit from colonial rule. For another example, IBM founder , Bill and Melinda Gates set up the Gates Foundation to help poor countries. We take a lot of things for granted. This cannot go on. A spirit of give-and-take is essential for world harmony. Developed countries may not be bound by law to help poor nations, but they have the responsibility - and the power - to do so.

However, developed countries should help less developed ones. But whether this is an obligation is a matter for debate. I believe the government of a country should be responsible for the well-being of its people. It is wrong to allow outsiders to influence the development of a country. This could lead to serious problems.

A developed country faces various difficulties when choosing who to help. First, its choice could leave a lot of people unhappy and damage its relationship with other countries. Second, allowing foreigners to have a significant influence on a nation could lead to negative consequences. Some donors do not have the best intentions. They could use their power for their own advantage. This could lead to corruption and financial loss in the less developed country. Third, a developing nation may become dependent on foreign aid. And some donors might charge a hefty interest for their financial assistance. This could pose a bigger headache than not receiving aid at all. Hence, rich countries have to be careful when helping poor nations. It involves a lot of politics so the rich have the right to choose the recipient and ensure the aid does not get into the wrong hands.

● Rich countries have responsibilites to assist global economy development or balance economy development

When global economy is unbalance developing. It will bring the damage of kindly cooperation relationship , e.g. export and import business activities to develop our global economy in success. For example, China and America themselve trade war will cause these both countries' GDP export and import income loss, even global economy will be recession. So, rich country, such as US has responsibility to assist developing country, such as Afria, China, Korea, Taiwan to help them to raise business competive effort and bring long term export and import business cooperation and create many factory jobs to China, Korea, Africa, Taiwan factory workers. Then, they can build kindly business cooperative relationship to bring global economy benefit in long term. Then, our global economy development will succeed more easily.

The first rational basis behind donating to poor countries is the notion that all men are equal. Some may radically oppose this concept, noting that their countries should solely invest its own efforts to remedy impoverished sectors of the population. Given the spread of poverty and homelessness, some have arrived to the conclusion that aiding other countries is not in our best interest. However, this could not be further from the truth. As member of the human race, we all occupy an equitable status as global citizens, and nothing can detract from this truth. Centralise your focus on the relative needs of your nation disregards the ailing needs of the developing world.

The second consideration simply poses the question of why not? Although wealthier, developed countries are plagued by their own respective incidences of poverty and lack of resources, developing countries suffer greatly, in terms of their accessibility to medical aid, vaccines, clean water, and a number of other amenities that are gravely understated in importance. With this said, we must venture beyond the bounds of our own comfort zones, and aid other countries because we are lavished with such a bounty in resources ourselves. Another indispensable benefit of aiding impoverished countries. Foreign diplomacy can significantly aid the national security of any nation. And providing aid to a poor county can ultimately benefit us, improving our perception in their eyes, a cultivating a certain level of civility and coexistence that breeds peace, instead of war. The fewer enemies that a particular nation has, the better.

The final reason is simple. We should empathize with other

human beings. Every day, countless children succumb to curable disease, malaria and a number of other pathogens that could easily be treated with outside aid. Both children and adults are sold into slavery and trafficked around the world. Of course, the lingering issue of starvation is a palpable one that still plagues the world today. With this said, we should uphold a noble standard that permits foreign aid for this very reason. One often hears the argument that it is all very well to preach equity but given the planetary emergency the world faces from the threat of climate change we must set aside the equity principle in the interests of humanity as a whole. This is a wholly specious and self serving argument. It reflects the sense of entitlement to an affluent lifestyle, based on energy intensive production and consumption, while denying the even modest aspirations of people in developing countries. For example, global climate changes to warmth challenge , it can cause developing countries people their health to be poor. In a densely interconnected and globalised world, it will be impossible to maintain islands of prosperity in an ocean of poverty and deprivation. It is not that developing countries are claiming the right to spew as much carbon as possible into the atmosphere without regard to the health of the planet. As the main victims of climate change– the impacts of which they are already suffering – they have a much bigger stake in dealing with this challenge. They are, in fact, doing much more than most developed countries, to adopt energy frugal methods of growth, conserving energy, promoting renewable power and limiting waste within the limits of their own resources.

Why and how developing countries people's poor health issue , it may influence developed countries businessmen income ? I shall indicate Africa , developing example , if

African are health, then this country will have many workers to assist or help US businessmen to manufacture many products to sell to different countries in short time. If US businessmen hope to pay the low wage to reduce their long time expenditure, Afrian must need have health to do any hard jobs in factories. If US businessmen only feel Chinese workers can help them to do any low wage jobs in factories, when China have many new businesses develop to pay better wages to employ themselves Chinese workers. Then, many Chinese workers may choose to help themselves China employers to do the factory jobs to replace US employers. So, if US can help many African have health to work, it may bring uncounted long time benefits to US businesses. Hence, such as this case, it explains why rich people need to help developing countries to solve health challenge.

Methods developing countries can
become developed countries

● Main industries aspects need to develop

How can developing countries develop to be developed countries in success? What the difficulties to them , that they will need to solve in this development process ? In today's sophisticated society,people of the developing countries are still fighting for their basic righs such a better healthcare,proper education and a sound source of income.While the governments of the underdeveloped countries are struggling to improve the living standards of their people,I believe that contribution by richer nations should be more in this regard. To begin,all human beings should help each other.Govenments of richer nations can take many steps to improve the living standard of the poorer naions. I shall indicate these aspects that they need to concentrate on solving in order to achieve developed countries in success as below:

(1) Healthcare development

Firstly,in the field of healthcare,developed countries can support he underdeveloped in many ways.They can send their expert doctors to train the medical staff in the developing countries.Also,they can open free medical camps in the selected areas of poor countries.In this way free medical advice could be given.Such camps can also start health awarness compaigns to make people aware of unhealthy lifetyle. Moreover, experts from the developed countries can also help with the vaccination programmes in the developing countries.This will led to decrease in infant mortality rate.

(2) Educational development

Secondly,assistance in the field of education should be provide to the poorer nations.The developed countries can provide funds to open new schools and polytechnic institutions.These will not only increase the literacy rate,but will also provide vocational education.Furthermore,the rich governments should provide the students of poor countries an oportunity to study in the prestigious institutions by giving scholarships.This will promote poor people to gain higher education.

(3) Promoting free trade development

Finally,rich nations should help to improve the economy of poor countries.This can be done by promoting free trade.This wil reduce barriers to international trade such as tariff,import quotas and export fee and will help to lift the developing countries out of poverty. To conclude,if we want to live in a beter world with peace and harmony,we should always help each other.Therefore,I believe that richer nations should help the poor countries in all the fields.

● The challenges are needed to solve in development process

During the development process, they developing countries will need to solve these challenges, the developing or underdeveloped countries (as they were earlier named) are poor due to them having the following common characteristics as below:

The developing countries may have these social challenges , they need to solve , such as :

(1) On social medical aspect

Closed economy/State Controlled economy or practice of socialism (which is in practice -one man/one party dictatorship). Low levels of literacy and esp. female literacy (less than 75% female literacy). Low health and HDI indicators (corresponding to the literacy levels). Low per capita income. High incidence of corruption, nepotism and kleptocracy.

The following is the path chosen by most of the former "low income/under developed/poor nations" to become developed (Germany & Japan post WW2, South Korea, Taiwan, Brazil, South Africa and China - some are still in process)- Economically liberal but politically/socially conservative regimes. Immense government spending (Keynesian economics) on - Infrastructure (Roads, Schools, Bridges, Ports, Airports, Power Plants, Hospitals and primary health centers etc).

(2) On international trade social aspect

Opening up the economy to international trade and foreign investments. Export oriented manufacturing practices, wherein the bulk of the population which was in the primary sector (agriculture, animal husbandry and mining etc) shifts to the secondary sector (manufacturing) and experiences corresponding increase in wages/income.

Application of procedures and rule of law on a gradual basis from the earlier arbitrariness which reigned supreme. The first step, in my view, is to make sure to have an honest and capable government that are committed to the development of the country and to the welfare of all people in the country. It is, in fact, the most difficult step to start with. Once we have a good and capable government, it is not so difficult to figure out or implement all steps necessary to make the country developed and prosper. On the other hand, having a corrupt, incapable, in other words, not only dishonest, but also stupid and foolish government means losing everything, no matter how abundance resource your country has, or how much foreign assistance and aids your country receives.

However, some economists believe that they are not "developing", but MAINTAINED IN PERMANENT UNDERDEVELOPMENT on purpose. Market, same as everything, functions in 3D, the 3rd is the income strata. The "progress" is not for all the strata. Every upper stratum solves its own problems at expenses of pushing the next inferior one downwards (vertically) or over the edge (horizontally). Spend a few minutes on a search engine and you realize that the term "first world" is meaningless when referring to economic development. For example, Ireland, Switzerland and Sweden are examples of third world countries. A first world nation is one that allied with NATO as opposed to the Soviet Union during the Cold War.

(3) On solving social poverty aspect

Poverty is the default state of man. Knowledge is what allows us to go beyond our physical and cognitive limitations. With knowledge you can create technology that makes our lives better. At a base level, developing nations need a smaller percentage of their populations working in sustenance farming. This could be achieved by increases in farming productivity which would allow other people to specialize in making other goods and providing other services. Essentially creating more wealth.

Uaually, developing countries lack enough farming technology, they can't specialize in something other than sustenance farming if 80% of your population farms with oxen instead of machines. This is where knowledge comes in play. Many developing nations have rich natural resources and commodities they just don't have the knowledge necessary to turn it into something useful.

To summarize in one word what is necessary for a developing nation to become a developed one it is knowledge. Any one developing countries need to answer these questions, before they decide how to solve these social challenges in their development process as below:

What developing country will become the next developed nation? Why do they are developing countries ? How can they develop to be developed countries ? How long will it take for every country in the world to become developed? What is the way to develop a country? Which countries are likely to be developed countries soon?

For example, Brazilians is one developing country, because this country has high crime rate and poor rate is high and inflation is high. These are its social problems. As soon as hyperinflation and out-of-control crime was solved, Brazilians brought their money back to Brazil. The starting point for Brazilians is patriotism and nostalgia. Even with all the problems of corruption, taxes, bureaucracy and poor infrastructure if given a chance to make real money within the country a Brazilian will leave better opportunities in the

US. So, Brazilians need to solve these social problems if this country hope to become one developed country in success. The easiest way to develop is: when each and every person decides to learn as much as possible, and decides to behave like civilized persons, who have total respect for all other persons' physical and patrimonial integrity. It's that easy and simple. But, often, the easiest things in life are the most difficult to learn.

● What a developing country should do to be a developed one?

The countries that developed the fastest often had the longest paths. If you compensate for that fact, then it becomes obvious that economic freedom is both necessary and sufficient. In particular, countries should avoid: socialism, i.e. collectivization of the means of production expropriation, i.e. robbing foreign investors of their properties autarchy, i.e. cutting all international trade. The less countries engage in these, the faster they develop.

● How can a developing country become a developed country?

Well, you could study economic history and learn how the present developed countries attained their present positions. There are also several examples in real time: look at how China and India are moving their countries from third world countries to developed economies. Two other interesting examples: Several African countries are using primarily cell phone techologies for communication and bypassing the infrastructure requirements for hardline technology. Ireland is well know to have been deforested when it's forests were harvested for the coal and fuel requirements of industrializing.

● Developed Countries need to help Developing Countries to increase their competitive effort in societies IMPROVEMENTS IN HEALTH, EDUCATION AND TRADE ARE ESSENTIAL FOR THE DEVELOPMENT OF POORER NATIONS. HOWEVER,THE GOVERNMENTS OF RICHER NATIONS SHOULD TAKE MORE RESPONSIBILITY FOR HELPING THE POORER NATIONS IN SUCH AREAS. Eliminate political tension by encouraging participation of all in the political, constitutional and economic processes. I recommend developed countries, such as US, UK can help developing countries to develop in sucess in these several aspects:

-Invest in infrastructure, education and health care.

-Encourage rural agriculture by providing agricultural inputs

and raising earned incomes.

-Raise levels of literacy

-Encourage the modern sectors of banking, manufacturing, retail,

and extractive industries,

-Provide adequate sanitation and clean water

-Open the countries to direct foreign investments

-Remove trade barriers to exports and imports.

-Reduce dependency on single sectors that is diversification .

Can bring global benefit when all countries are developed countries

1. How Globalization Affects Developed Countries There are three perspective of globalization. Which are as : The Hyper globalist perspective: This says that economies are becoming Denationalized due to this government will lose it influence over the trade within its border. It will

have both good and bad effects. The Skeptical perspective: it is kind based on myth that globalization will not help the under develop country as they do not perform a greater role in flow of trade and services in the global economy.

I assume that future one day, all countries can become developed countries. The globalization development effect will be caused by our global successful development. Does it means that globalization can only bring benefits ? I shall explain that when all countries can developed successfully. Globalization ought not only bring benefits to our global societies as below:

Globalization brings people and businesses together through the international exchange of money, ideas, and culture. However, some critics say it adversely affects developed countries. Opinions exist on both sides of the globalization debate. Proponents claim lower opportunity costs, producing positive growth, and reduced market volatility. At the same time, opponents decry the reduction of domestic job growth, cost of mismanagement to countries and the world, and the stagnation of wages.

Conflicting Globalization Views

U.S. President Donald Trump, for example, has been very vocal on his views of globalization and has taken a protectionist stance when it comes to free trade under agreements like the North American Free Trade Agreement (NAFTA), calling for higher taxes on imports and fewer multinational trade agreements. He has also increased tariffs on foreign goods to discourage their importation and use. No matter how much economists are quick to extol the universal benefits of globalization, some politicians and other economist demonize globalization as a force that takes away domestic jobs. These conflicting viewpoints have created a maelstrom of opinions and policies across developed countries that range from extreme protectionism through trade barriers, like President Trump's example, to complete openness.

From an economic standpoint, globalization is typically defined as the increase in the global trade of goods, services, capital, and technology. This growth in trade has been especially acute between developed countries like the United States and emerging markets, such as China. There are many factors behind the increase in global trade. European devastation after World War I and II helped to jumpstart America and an industrial superpower and exporter. Lower transportation costs have reduced the costs of trade, technologies have eliminated some barriers altogether, and liberal economic policies have helped lower political barriers to trade. While cost reductions have helped accelerate trade, the largest driver behind global trade is supply-demand economics and the desire to increase consumption on the part of both importers and exporters.

Benefits of globalization

The core benefit of globalization is the comparative advantage—that is, the ability of one country to produce goods or services at a lower opportunity cost than other countries. While the idea seems simple on the surface, it quickly becomes counterintuitive when examined more deeply. The theory suggests that two countries capable of producing two commodities at different costs can benefit the most by exporting the good where the comparative advantage exists. For example, a developing country may have a comparative advantage in producing cement, and the United States may have a comparative advantage in producing semiconductors. While the U.S. may be able to produce cement more efficiently than the developing country, the U.S. would still be better off focusing on semiconductors because of its comparative advantage. This is why globalization is powerful as a driver of global consumption between countries of all capabilities.

One of the major potential benefits of globalization is to provide opportunities for reducing macroeconomic volatility on output and consumption via diversification of risk. The overall evidence of the globalization effect on macroeconomic volatility of output indicates that although direct effects are ambiguous in theoretical models, financial integration helps in a nation's production base diversification, and leads to an increase in specialization of production. However, the specialization of production, based on the concept of comparative advantage, can also lead to higher volatility in specific industries within an economy and society of a nation. As time passes, successful companies, independent of size, will be the ones that are part of the global economy.

Empirical evidence suggests that a positive growth effect takes place in countries that are sufficiently rich when it comes to globalization. For investors and economies, globalization also provides the opportunity to reduce the volatility of output and consumption, since products and services can be imported or exported with greater ease. Fewer "bubbles" arise from a mismatch in supply and demand if the production of goods and services is more elastic. But, when all countries can develop to become developed countries, globalization developed countries which may also bring these disadvantages as below:

Drawbacks of globalization

Globalization is often criticized for taking away jobs from domestic companies and workers. After all, the U.S. cement industry will go out of business if imports from a developing country drive down prices, even if consumption increases. Small U.S. cement companies would find it difficult to compete and likely shut down, leaving workers unemployed, while the larger U.S. cement industry would likely experience a significant protracted decline.

A second criticism is the high cost of a comparative or absolute advantage to a country's own well-being if mismanaged. For example, China has become a leading worldwide emitter of carbon dioxide thanks to its comparative advantage in manufacturing a wide range of products. Other countries may have a comparative advantage in mining certain natural resources—such as crude oil—and mishandle the revenue generated from those activities.

A final disadvantage of globalization is the increase in wages for workers, which can hurt corporate profitability. For example, if a rich country has a high comparative advantage in developing software, they may drive up the price of software engineers around the world, which makes it difficult for foreign companies to compete in the market. The phenomenon of globalization began in a primitive form when humans first settled into different areas of the world; however, it has shown a rather steady and rapid progress in recent times and has become an international dynamic which, due to technological advancements, has increased in speed and scale, so that countries in all five continents have been affected and engaged.

What Is Globalization? Why and how globalization may achieve when global countries can develop to become developed countries ?

Globalization is defined as a process that, based on international strategies, aims to expand business operations on a worldwide level, and was precipitated by the facilitation of global communications due to technological advancements, and socioeconomic, political and environmental developments.

The goal of globalization is to provide organizations a superior competitive position with lower operating costs, to gain greater numbers of products, services, and consumers. This approach to competition is gained via diversification of resources, the creation and development of new investment opportunities by opening up additional markets and accessing new raw materials and resources. Diversification of resources is a business strategy that increases the variety of business products and services within various organizations. Diversification strengthens institutions by lowering organizational risk factors, spreading interests in different areas, taking advantage of market opportunities, and acquiring companies both horizontal and vertical in nature.

Industrialized or developed nations are specific countries with a high level of economic development and meet certain socioeconomic criteria based on economic theory, such as gross domestic product (GDP), industrialization and human development index (HDI) as defined by the International Monetary Fund (IMF), the United Nations (UN) and the World Trade Organization (WTO). Using these definitions, some industrialized countries are: United Kingdom, Belgium, Denmark, Finland, France, Germany, Japan, Luxembourg, Norway, Sweden, Switzerland, and the United States.

Components of Globalization

The components of globalization include GDP, industrialization and the Human Development Index (HDI). The GDP is the market value of all finished goods and services produced within a country's borders in a year and serves as a measure of a country's overall economic output. Industrialization is a process which, driven by technological innovation, effectuates social change and economic development by transforming a country into a modernized industrial, or developed nation. The Human Development Index comprises three components: a country's population's life expectancy, knowledge and education measured by the adult literacy, and income.

The degree to which an organization is globalized and diversified has bearing on the strategies that it uses to pursue greater development and investment opportunities. When all countries can become developed countries. They may bring the Economic Impact on Developed Nations as below: Globalization compels businesses to adapt to different strategies based on new ideological trends that try to balance the rights and interests of both the individual and the community as a whole. This change enables businesses to compete worldwide and also signifies a dramatic change for business leaders, labor and management by legitimately accepting the participation of workers and government in developing and implementing company policies and strategies. Risk reduction via diversification can be accomplished through company involvement with international financial institutions and partnering with both local and multinational businesses. Globalization brings reorganization at the international, national and sub-national levels. Specifically, it brings the reorganization of production, international trade and the integration of financial markets. This affects capitalist economic and social relations, via multilateralism and microeconomic phenomena, such as business competitiveness, at the global level. The transformation of production systems affects the class structure, the labor process, the application of technology and the structure and organization of capital. Globalization is now seen as marginalizing the less educated and low-skilled workers. Business expansion will no longer automatically imply increased employment. Additionally, it can cause a high remuneration of capital, due to its higher mobility compared to labor.

The phenomenon seems to be driven by three major forces: the globalization of all product and financial markets, technology, and deregulation. Globalization of product and financial markets refers to an increased economic integration in specialization and economies of scale, which will result in greater trade in financial services through both capital flows and cross-border entry activity. The technology factor, specifically telecommunication and information availability, has facilitated remote delivery and provided new access and distribution channels, while revamping industrial structures for financial services by allowing entry of non-bank entities, such as telecoms and utilities.

When all countries can become developed countries. In a global economic view, power is the ability of a company to command both tangible and intangible assets that create customer loyalty, regardless of location. Independent of size or geographic location, a company can meet global standards and tap into global networks, thrive and act as a world-class thinker, maker, and trader, by using its greatest assets: its concepts, competence, and connections. When all developing countries become developed countries, they may bring these beneficial effects as below:

Some economists have a positive outlook regarding the net effects of globalization on economic growth. These effects have been analyzed over the years by several studies attempting to measure the impact of globalization on various nations' economies using variables such as trade, capital flows, and their openness, GDP per capita, foreign direct investment (FDI) and more. These studies examined the effects of several components of globalization on growth using time-series cross-sectional data on trade, FDI and portfolio investment. Although they provide an analysis of individual components of globalization on economic growth, some of the results are inconclusive or even contradictory. However, overall, the findings of those studies seem to be supportive of the economists' positive position, instead of the one held by the public and non-economist view.

Trade among nations via the use of comparative advantage promotes growth, which is attributed to a strong correlation between the openness to trade flows and the effect on economic growth and economic performance. Additionally, there is a strong positive relation between capital flows and their impact on economic growth. Foreign Direct Investment's impact on economic growth has had a positive growth effect in wealthy countries and an increase in trade and FDI, resulting in higher growth rates.8 Empirical research examining the effects of several components of globalization on growth, using time series and cross-sectional data on trade, FDI and portfolio investment, found that a country tends to have a lower degree of globalization if it generates higher revenues from trade taxes. Further evidence indicates that there is a positive growth-effect in countries that are sufficiently rich, as are most of the developed nations.

The World Bank reports that integration with global capital markets can lead to disastrous effects, without sound domestic financial systems. One of the potential benefits of globalization is to provide opportunities for reducing macroeconomic volatility on output and consumption via diversification of risk.

However, when all countries can become developed countries, they may also bring these harmful effects as below:

Non-economists and the wide public expect the costs associated with globalization to outweigh the benefits, especially in the short-run. Less wealthy countries from those among the industrialized nations may not have the same highly-accentuated beneficial effect from globalization as more wealthy countries, measured by GDP per capita, etc. Although free trade increases opportunities for international trade, it also increases the risk of failure for smaller companies that cannot compete globally. Additionally, free trade may drive up production and labor costs, including higher wages for a more skilled workforce, which again can lead to outsourcing jobs from countries with higher wages. Moreover, domestic industries in some countries may be endangered due to comparative or absolute advantage of other countries in specific industries. Another possible danger and harmful effect is the overuse and abuse of natural resources to meet new higher demands in the production of goods.

In overall, when all countries can develop to become developed countries, they may bring these general benefits to influence our society to bring positive changes. They may include: Globalization activity doesn't only reduce trade boundary but it lot more effects like one country come closer to the economy of other country, it help in mixture of culture, it helps in transfer information and technology, increase group of buyer and seller of products and services etc. this are only few advantages of globalizations. Due to globalization trade is getting more interdependent and to protect interest of every nation W.T.O keep a close look over the trade of every nation. Due globalization many environmental threats are evolved every country is moving toward industrialization which increase global warming and it is needed to be checked. Social problem are also occurred like exploitation of labour, increase in child labour in developing nations, lack of powerful labour union etc this social problem are needed to taken care of and proper law should be made to avoid such kind of problems. As every things as has some advantages, it also has some disadvantages also.

Advantages:
- New market for product.
- Helps in growth of economy.
- Increase in infrastructure.
- Free flow of technology and information.
- Reduction in poverty.
- Increases in employments.
- International body governs trade through its law, so interest of every country should be protected.

Disadvantages are as follows:
- It brings competitions because of which small scale industries suffer in under develop countries.
- Globalization lead to growth in infrastructure but on other hand it bring harm to environment due to industrialization, reduction in forest areas.
- Due to globalization environment, labour, resource of under develop countries are exploited by develop countries.
- Poor trade union.
- Lack of control over country economy by its governments.

Effect of globalization on developing countries or third world countries

The thinking of first world, second world and third world countries are given by U.S.A which place itself as the first world nation, European countries as second world nations and as far as third world country are concerned under develop and developing countries come under this categories. The third world countries are further classified as under developed countries and developing countries. In under developed, countries like Afghanistan, Nepal, Bangladesh, Nigeria, Bhutan, Pakistan etc comes this are the growing nations but as far as development of economy is concerned they are far behind. In developing countries, countries like China, India, South Africa, Brazil etc are included because this are among fastest growing nation after globalization has taken place. But under develop countries are not much benefited because of this globalization process. Rather than getting benefit they are exploited. In a sense, due to cheap labour these countries manpower is exploited and it natural resource is been taken away as we can take the example of china, china is investing a lot in African nation and on exchange of this it is utilizing its natural resources.

What influences to the countries like china and India has grown tremendously after globalization.

Before globalizations export of china was not very high but now it is one the global leader in exports and as far as India is concerned before India was accounted only for 0.6 % of world export and now it is accounted for 1 % of world exports. Brazil has also show huge growth its per capita income has also increased. Countries like Bhutan, Malaysia, Indonesia etc has tremendous growth in GDP in past five years. Outsourcing has increased in these nations. Now India earns 51% of GDP from service sectors and its service sector is growing tremendously because of it excellence in IT sectors and this boosted up after globalizations. Now china earns major part of it GDP from export which increased after globalization. As far as Latin America is concerned Brazil has show tremendous growth in export, technology and manufacturing sectors. And now it is among top five of developing nations.

Effect of globalization on developed countries when all developing countries can become developed countries

Due to globalization the develop countries are moving towards underdeveloped countries like India, China, Indonesia etc for outsourcing their job to these countries because of cheap labour. Nowadays develop nation are coming to under develop nation for setting up manufacturing plants in these nation because of its availability of cheap and skilled labours. Due to globalization develop countries are facing intense competition from underdeveloped countries, competition in sense employment, exports, technology etc. Due to globalization developed countries are also exploit resources like natural resource, manpower, and environment etc. of underdeveloped nations. Also, due to globalization the dominance of developed nation is also reducing. The people of developed nation are facing intense competition for job from people growing nation like china, India, Thailand etc. now for FDI in developed nation are reducing due increase in the FDI in developing countries like china, Brazil, India etc. Thus, when all developing countries can develop to become developed countries in future one day. Globalization developed countries got new market for their products and services, and new place for their business expansions.

Development of "Regional economic" will truly help India to build viable economic future for its citizens.

Due to globalization various effect and development has take place which help india to build viable economic future for its citizens. Due Globalization to this the infrastructure of India has developed a lot because of which transportation, sanitary, hygiene, sports complex and stadium has developed a lot and still developing which will give better environment for future generation. Nowadays, foreign education institutes are coming to india which has increased the level of education. Export of india is increasing with each quarter which help to reduce the fiscal deficit and increase the GDP of the nation.

Nowadays more and more manufacturing industries are established because of which more employment is created and hence improving per capita income of the nation. Due globalization India is more concerned about the global warming and planning its growth in such a way that it could reduce it contribution in global. And it will be helpful for future citizens.

Regional economies help to reduce domination of developed economies on the developing economies.

Developments in regional economy will strength the self reliability of the nation which will help to reduction in the dependence on other nation. Development of regional economy will lead to increase in GDP, Standard of living, Per capita income of the nation. If India wants to emerge as supper power it has to develop it regional because it is the stepping stone toward it.

In conclusion, when all countries can develop to achieve developed countries. They will create development of regional economy to our global societies. Then, they may bring these benefits in possible. They may include: Development of regional economy will lead to reduce in inequalities of distribution of wealth, development of regional economy will lead to increase in metropolitan culture, development of regional economy will lead increase the contributions of every state in Indian GDP, development of regional economy will lead to reduction of poverty, unemployment and illiteracy.

2. Economic growth advantages and disadvantages

When all developing countries can develop to be developed countries, then it may also bring global economic growth. However, I believe that when global societies can have sudden economic growth in short time, due to all or many developing countries can develop to be developed countries in success. They may bring advantages and disadvantages both aspects as below:

Economic development can be describe as the development of economic wealth of countries or regions for the well-being of their inhabitants such as the improvement and innovation on the political, economic, and social of its people. Economic development and growth are totally different in terms which are used in economics. Economic development refers to economic growth which accompanied by changes in economic structure and output distribution. So, economic growth may be necessary but not sufficient to attain economic development. Thus, peoples always said that economic development is the problems of underdeveloped countries and economic growth to those of developed countries. Underdeveloped countries always face some problems such as low income, weakness of human resource and also the economic vulnerability. These problems also made the countries hard to attain the development of economic. However, for those developed countries, they do not face the same problems as what underdeveloped countries do, therefore, they are more easily to attain the economic development and treat it as an economic growth.

In addition, in the term of economic development is much more comprehensive because it implies progressive changes in the socio-economic structure of a country. Nowadays, the evolution of new technology is directly related to economic development. Without high technology in a country, it is hard to bring an economic development toward its people. Viewed in this way economic development involves a steady decline in agricultural shares in GNP and continuous increase in shares of industries, trade banking construction and services. However, economic growth just only refers to the rise in total output in a country; development implies change in technological and institutional organization of production as well as in distributive pattern of income. Hence, if compared to the goal of development, economic growth is much easy to realize. Between, we just need a larger mobilization of resources and raising their productivity by enhance it to be more efficiency and effective, then the output level can be raised and economic growth will occur. However, the development process is far more extensive than the economic growth. Not only a rise in output, it also involved changes in composition of output, and shift in the allocation of productive resources, and reduction or elimination of poverty, inequalities and unemployment. However, economic development is impossible without having an economic growth but economic growth is possible without an economic development. Growth is just increase in GNP but it does not have any other parameters to it; unlike development which can be conceived as Multi-

Dimensional process.

Are economic growth and development worthwhile? Economic growth and development have their advantages and also disadvantages. Although economic growth widens the range of human choices, but this may not necessarily bring happiness toward people. Happiness is dependent on the relationship between wants and resources. People may become more satisfied, not only by having more wants met, but perhaps also by renouncing certain material goods. Wealth may make people less happy if it increases wants more than resources. Furthermore, acquisitive and achievement-oriented societies may be more likely to give rise to individual frustration.

Advantages

Economic growth will decreases famine, starvation, infant mortality, and death; gives us greater leisure; can enhance art, music, and philosophy; and gives us the resources to be humanitarian. Economic growth will especially benefit to societies in which political desire exceed the resources, because it may prevent what might otherwise prove to be social tension that people can't take it. However, without economic growth, the desires of one group can be met when others expense on it. Lastly, economic growth can help newly independent countries in mobilizing resources to increase the power of a nation.

Disadvantages

Growth has its value. First, the disadvantage might be the acquisitiveness, materialism, and dissatisfaction with one's present state associated with a society's economic struggles. Second, liquidity, objective, and self-associated with economic growth may undermine the reliance on extended family system, in fact, the focus of the prevailing social structure. Third, economic growth, which depends on the rational and technological innovation and changes in scientific methods, often is the threat in religious and social authority. Fourth, economic growth often require more specialized work, which may be caused by more objective, accompanied more drab and monotonous tasks, more discipline, and a pair of process loss.

In addition, economic growth which follow by large organizational units are more likely to lead to bureaucratization, objective, communication problems, and the use of force were consistent. Economic growth and development of large enterprises with a manufacturer's products and services while demand increased, and urban growth, this may be is accompanied byrootlessness, environmental blight disease, and unhealthy living conditions, even in the narrow social values change and may ultimately lead to a new dynamic equilibrium that is better than the old static equilibrium, the transition could have some very painful issues. In addition, the political transformation, as rapid economic growth, may lead to greater concentration, stress, social disruption, even authoritarian. Therefore, even if the population seriously committed to economic growth, its implementation is not likely at all costs pursued. All societies must take into account that the conflicts with the maximization of economic growth and other objectives. Because it was want sits in high level positions, a developing country own citizens can promote the local production control to reduce the growth in the short term.

The question now is what will be weighed to achieve an orderly, stable society, and maintain traditional values and culture, and promoting political autonomy? Economic growth is the increase a country's per capita output.

Economic development, economic growth has resulted in the poorest strata of the population or level of education, changes to improve the output distribution of economic welfare and economic changes in different structures.

Economic growth and development of Asia when all or many developing countries can develop to be developed countries

Nowadays, economic development in Asia shows high impact of economic development of this respective continent. Economy of Asia has taken an important part in the view of the world's economy. These continents have adopted one of the following economic systems such as capitalism, socialism, communism, and fascism. As we know, Asia is the largest continent in terms of area surface and also the population. Beside it, it is also the region with the highest growth rate. Below are Asian countries that contribute their economic development to our society.

Of all the Asian Countries, the only Asian country included among the industrialized countries is Japan. According to the International Monetary Fund, the country per capita was GDP 32,608 U.S. dollars or in 2009, the 23rd highest on record. Moreover, according to certain criteria, the term means that developed countries is the countries that having a high level of development. What standards and which countries are classified as being developed, is a controversial issue which surrounded by a fierce debate. Thus, economic criteria tend to dominate discussions. Countries which having per capita income and high per capita gross domestic product (GDP) will be described as developed countries. Another criterion is the industrialization; countries in the tertiary and quaternary sector-of industry leading will be described as development. Another recent measure, the human development index, which combines economic measures, and other measures of national income, life expectancy and education indicators, have become prominent. This criterion will define the development country as those very high (HDI) rating. However, many exceptions exist when the decision to "developed country" status is used to measure the subject. Countries do not fit this definition are classified as developing countries.

However, Taiwan, Hong Kong and Singapore are regarded as newly industrialized countries. The category of newly industrialized country (NIC) is a socioeconomic classification which applied to various countries in the world by political scientists and economists. NIC is the nation's economy has not yet reached first world status, but in the macro sense, the development of the countries is normally faster than counterpart. Another feature of newly industrialized countries is that undergoing in rapid economic growth (usually export-oriented). However, the starting or ongoing industrialization is an important indicator of NIC. In many newly industrialized countries, may also be experiencing social unrest by major primary rural, or agricultural, populations migrate to the cities, where the thousand of laborers can be draw by growth of manufacturing concerns and factories. In the social development process, it usually shares some characteristic such as increased social freedoms and civil rights, strong political leadership, which switch from an agricultural to an industrial economy, the other common features, especially in the manufacturing sector, an increasingly open market economy with free trade and other heavy capital investment from countries around the world. In addition, the political leadership in their area of influence and lastly is they have lowered poverty rates.

I shall indicate China, Philippines, India, North Korea these developing country when they can become developed country , what it can bring global social change influence example. Moreover, as we know, the history and culture of China is their secret to improve their economy, even if it ruled and control by their state. Prior to 1979, China maintained a centrally planned or command economy. The economy of China with the large proportion is directed by the state which established production goals, controlled prices, distribution, and most of the economic control of resources. During the 1950s, all of China's individual household farms were collectivized into large communes. To support rapid industrialization, the central government starts to take large-scale physical and human capital investment during 1960-1970s. As a result, by 1978, nearly three quarters of industrial production generated by the central control of state-owned enterprises according to centrally planned output targets. Private enterprises and foreign invested enterprises are almost non-existent.

A central objective of Chinese government was to make China's economy relatively self-sufficient. Foreign trade was generally limited to those commodity which unable to obtain or receive the goods in China. The Government's policy to keep the Chinese economy relatively stagnant and inefficient, mainly because of where the profits of some enterprises and farmers to stimulate competition, in fact, does not exist, price and production controls caused widespread economic distortions. China's standard of living is much lower than those of many other.

In addition, India is contributing in business process outsourcing improvement for the information technology which has a significant impact for the economic development in South Asia. The Philippines is improving, because they help to remittances from abroad, they send money to their loved ones from overseas Filipino workers to improve their country. North Korea shows hammer and sling as a symbol for their communistic views of their economic system in Far East Asia. While South Korea shows modern technology that is influence from Western countries which results an improvement of technology in their designated countries. Indonesia is a Muslim country, the whole of Asia's largest population by the Dutch colony. It is based on their banking and finance in the Islamic way of life. This is also the case in Malaysia was a British colony. After analyze the information of some Asian Countries, I discovered that they are facing several problems in economic development. First, they have low standard of living, low level of production, there is a rapid population growth, they having a high rate of unemployment, lastly, there are over dependence on agricultural production and exportation of raw materials and also the international trade.

Economic growth and development of Malaysia
According to the recent The Star's newspaper, Malaysia economic development is one of fastest and steady in global economic scenario. Malaysia GDP per capita has been estimated to be $15,700 in fiscal year 2008. This is a clear indication of tremendous economic development in Malaysia. Malaysia economy is a middle income country that has developed since 1970's. It was previously a mere raw materials producing economy, which has evolved now as a developing multi-sector economy. This growth bears testimony to impressive economic development at Malaysia. Prime Minister Abdullah, after coming to power in 2003, has tried to develop economy of this south Asian country by introducing value added production. He took

a number of measures to introduce hi-tech technologies and encouraged investments in high technology industries, medical technology and pharmaceuticals. Efforts have been made by government of Malaysia to stop its dependence on export products. However, exports of electronics goods have always been a major factor in Malaysia economy. There has been huge profit accrued from export of oil and gas and it has been a major factor for Malaysia economic development. There have been huge profits from high energy prices, although there was high cost of gasoline and diesel fuel. This, however, made Kuala Lumpur minimize financial assistance of government. It has been found that currency value of Malaysia has hiked 6 percent per year when pitted against dollar in fiscal years 2006 to 2008.

Model of economy development: The production function how can be influenced to change when many or all developing countries can become developed countries

In macroeconomics, the production function is a function which specifies combination of all input from the output. In the macro-economy, production functions are functions that determine the output of a company which entered all combinations of input. A meta-production function comparing the practices of companies that has to change input to output to determine the function of the most efficient production practices of the entity that is, whether the most efficient production practices that qualify or production practices that are actually the most efficient. In these cases, the maximum output production process technology is defined as mathematical function of one or more entered. In other words, given a collection of all technical combination allows the output and input, just include a combination of maximum output for a given set of inputs to the production or function. Production function can be defined as specification of minimum input requirements needed to produce a total output that was, by given current technology. It is usually assumed that the production of unique functions can be built for every production technology.

Assuming when many or all developing countries can develop to become developed countries in future one day, they may bring these influences to our social technologic production function changes as below:

The maximum output possible from the set of technology inputs of all, the economic use in the production function analysis is the abstract essence of the technical and managerial problems associated with a specific production process. Engineering and managerial problems of technical competence is assumed to be broken, so the analysis can focus on the problem of efficiency allocate. States are assumed to make choices about how much each input of allocate factors put to use and how much output to produce, remember the cost (purchase price) of each factor, the sale price of output, and the factors represent technology to determine its production function. Frame results in one or more constant input can be used, for example, capital can be assumed to be fixed (constant) in the short term, and labor and possibly other variables such as input raw material, while in the long run, the quantity of capital and the factors that can be made by the company are variable. In the long term, companies may even have the choice of technology, represented by the various functions of production as possible.

Input to output relationship is non-financial, that the production function relating physical inputs to physical outputs, and prices and the cost is reflected in the function.

But the production function is not a complete model of the production process: intentionally abstract from the inherent aspects of physical production process that some would consider extremely important, including error, entropy or waste. In addition, the production functions do not typically model business processes, well, ignoring the role of management. (For primer on the basic elements of the production of Microeconomics theory, see production theory policies).

The main purpose of the production function is to address allocate efficiency in the use of input factors in production and distribution of factory income such factors. Based on certain assumptions, the production function can be used to reduce a marginalized product for each factor, which implies an ideal division of the revenue generated from the output to the income from their every input factor of production.

How global developed economy influences household expenditure decision?

In the saving function, there is a mathematical relation between saving and income by the household sector. Thus, the saving function can be stated as an equation such as a simple linear equation or a diagram indicated as the saving line. This function captures the relationship between savings and income, one of the other sides the relationship between consumer incomes, constitutes a cornerstone of Keynesian economics. The two key function to save the parameters are intercept, which indicates that self-saving, side slope, which is the marginal propensity to save, show that the induced savings. The injection- leakage model used in Keynesian economics is based on the saving function. Saving function on Keynesian economics is the starting point for determination of equilibrium output injection, leakage model. It captures the household sector in which the relationship between savings and income. As the income for either consumption or savings to use, saving feature is the complementary consumption function. Reflects the fundamental psychological law put forward by John Maynard Keynes, consumer spending (and saving by the household sector) depends on the income and just some of the revenue is used for consumption and saving the rest. This function is presented either as a mathematical formula, usually as a simple linear equation, graph or savings line. In either form, income is a measure of disposable income, national income and GDP. However, the saving function makes it easy to divide saving into two basic types such as the autonomous saving and Induced saving. Autonomous saving is the intercept term. Induced saving is the slope. Lastly, the slope of marginal propensity to save (MPS) also considered as saving function

How global developed economy influences the labor supply function changes ?

In mainstream economic theory, labor supply is the total number of hours number of a workers want to work in a given real wage rate. From the diagram above, we can see the positive relationship between the wages rate and also the quantity of labor. When the wage rate is low, the quantity of the labor also is low. However, when there is a rose in wage rate will also increase the quantity of labor. Realistically, the labor supply is the role of various factors within an economy. For example, as a heavy increased of population will make downward pressure on wages which may lead to high unemployment.

How global developed economy influences wage rate versus labor leisure changes?

Labor supply curves are derived from the 'labor-leisure' trade-off. More hours worked earn higher incomes but necessitate a cut in the amount of leisure that workers enjoy. Therefore, there are two aspects

to provide the necessary amount of labor is due to changes in real wage rates. For example, the real wage rate raises the opportunity cost of leisure increases as the diagram shows above. This tends to cause workers to supply more labor (the "substitution effect"). However, as the real wage rate rises, workers earn a higher income for a given number of hours. If leisure is a normal good – the demand for it increases as income increases – this increase in income will tend to cause workers to supply less labor (the "income effect"). If the "substitution effect" is stronger than the "income effect" then the labor supply curve will be upward sloping and vice versa.

However, from the view of Marxist, a labor supply is a core requirement in a capitalist society. In order to avoid Labor shortage and ensure a labor supply, a large portion of the population must not possess sources of self-provisioning, which would allow them to be independent, and they must instead be compelled, in order to survive, to sell their labor for a subsistence wage.

Economic development theories: Harrod-Domar theory When all or many countries can develop to be developed countries, how they can influence global technological growth rate changes. The Harrod-Domar theory delineates a functional economic relationship in which the growth rate of gross domestic product (g) depends directly on the national saving ratio (s) and inversely on the national capital/output ratio (k) so that it is written a $g = s / k$. The equation takes its name from a synthesis of analyses of growth process by two economists (Sir Roy Harrod of

Britain and E.V. Domar of the USA). The Harrod-Domar model in the early postwar times was commonly used by developing countries in economic planning. With a target growth rate, the required saving rate is known. If the country is not capable of generating that level of saving, a justification or an excuse for borrowing from international agencies can be established. An example in the Asian context is to ascertain the relationship between high growth rates and high saving rates in the cases of Japan and China. It is more difficult to introduce the third building block of a growth model, the labor and population element. In the long run, growth rate is constrained by population growth and also by the rate of technological change.

● Climate change will impact developed countries to continue develop

Will developed countries become
developing countries

● Why does illness can cause global economic recession to developed countries

Firstly, I shall explain why unpredicted illness factor can cause developed countries' economic recession. Although developed countries have advantages and let people to believe that their any medical, economic, education, business etc. different industries aspects are developed in mature. Their these any industries aspects are better or are improved better to compare the developing countries. But, in fact, whether it is possible that their any industries aspects will become worse to compare developing countries when they do not continue to improve any one of their industries aspects. I shall indiate whether what factors my cause developed countries to become developing countries in possible.

Many developing countries are facing problem very different from that of the developed countries. Countries such as Japan, Germany are facing depleting population whether on the other side countries like India, Indonesia are facing severe resource crunch due to population explosion. In such situation measuring the progress of the countries on the same scales decided by developed industrialized world is injustice to these countries. Developed world have achieved there parameters after journey of around 200-250 years post industrialization while many developing countries are in their 60s-70s after getting freedom from crutches of colonialism. In such cases developing countries should formulate their own parameters for growth and development and continue their progress. So, it seems that any developing countries will have possible to develop to be better any developed countries. Otherwise, any developed countries will have possible to bring worse development when they have many people loss jobs. For example, US economy will go down nowadays, due to the Chinese serious illness influences many US people die. Many US businessmen can not continue to manufacture or sell their products because many people can not go to offices or factories to work. They need to stay at homes to avoid the illness attacks when they need to contact the illness people in workplace, or they are walking on streets, or they are catching any public transport. So,although US is one developed country, but it can not still to avoid this China illness attack. It is possible due to US government neglects to consider this China illness is one kind of death sick to cause US has many people to die easily in this year 2020. If US government can prohibit to let Chinese travellers to enter its country when China has occurred this serious illness caused in 2019 last year. These Chiness illness people can not enter US to cause this kind of illness to attack any US people lung to cause they die. After it is possible that US can avoid to cause many US people to die. So, it does not consider whether the country is developed or not to avoid global economic recession, because it is illness factor to cause developed countries' economic recession, such as US, UK nowadays economic recession.

● Increasing social crime rate and government assistance may cause developed countries to become developing coutries

Secondly, I shall explain why increasing social crime rate or many young people do criminal behaviors in society, it can influence developed countries to develop worse or can not develop better in its society. Otherwise, when on developing countries have less crime rate or decreases its crime rate, it can develop better or improve its society to be better. For a developing country to catch up to a developed country, it must not only grow, but grow faster than the developed country. While It is possible for such accelerated growth to occur through rapid industrialization, but there are many country-specific factors that directly affect a developing country's ability to catch up to developed countries. They range from growth of productivity, labour force participation rate, standard of living, infrastructure, political environment etc.

For example, when the developing country can improve its education quality to let many young people learn any kinds of new knowledge to like do any kinds of jobs, even, driving

, factory labor, waiters, etc. low educational level jobs in society. Then, it will reduce its crime rate when many young people feel need to work. They won't need government to assist their life. Consequently, it will have possible to develop its economy or improve its economy to be better. In education primarily is the most essential quality that helps to empower the people of the country to communicate and achieve a common objective and is thus an extremely important driver for the developing to developed country journey. This is a common observation in all the developing countries. The one area that is still a struggle is education. Also, lack of education leads to increased poverty and disparity of income which leads to the 2nd most hindrance in a countries journey to achieve a developed nation status. Maybe if the path chosen is that of streamlining lack of education, poverty, a more driven and focused effort with individuals who know and can fathom the importance of this change working towards achieving a developed nation status can be undertaken. A semi-industrial, pro-human development approach should be a path adopted to see a qualitative shift in reducing this gap.

All through our education we have learnt 'India is a developing country' which brings to thought, will it ever be recognized as a 'developed country'? And what is the criteria to qualify as a developed nation? Are these criteria set by the developed nations to meet their convenience? If this is the case it would be more logical for developing nations to set their own criteria. It gets very difficult for developing nations to meet the criteria set by the giant economies, as even a single step gone wrong could ruin the effort of years. India can be seen as an example, where the step of demonetization and GST together led to a growth rate of 5.7%, weakest growth rate since the first quarter of

2014. These steps would probably have a positive effect in the long run and it is worth the wait. Another question to bring our attention to is, are the developed countries developed in the true sense? Considering the parameter of crime rate, USA has a very high crime rate. Another aspect could be unemployment, again US has a good percent of unemployed individuals every year. So, aren't the developed nations also falling short? It may be a good strategy for developing nations could be establishing a path which would help them use their resources aptly and generate output for their people.

In this race of matching with the developed nations we are leading nowhere, better we set a different goal all together. Every nation has a different potential given different kinds of resources they possess hence expecting the same output from all makes little sense. Hope the coming generation gets to learn, 'India is a developed country in the true sense'. Hence, high crime rate, such as US has high crime rate. Because it has many young people do not like to work, they depend on government assistance. Then, any kinds of low skill or low educational level job employers will feel difficult to find them to work. Then, their society will cause low skillful labour shortage challange. It is not due to US lacks enough low skill or low educational workers, it is due to they do not like to work, they feel wages are less , when their government can give any money or loss job allowance to support their lives in long time. It can enough these low educational level or low skillful level young people choose not work. Then, this US developed country will not have any young people to do any service job, e.g. driving public transport, waiter, security. When these kinds of job old people need to retire, these employers can not find any young people to replace them to do these service jobs. They can only choose to employ another old age people to replace the retired service staffs. Then, these kinds any one of service jobs can not raise their service level, their service performance will be worse or keep the same service level, it means that their performance can not perform better level to serve their clients in US society. It implies that developed country, such as US its general social service level will be worse or they can not be improved to satisfy their client needs. In this developed country's poor service environment, how to explain it can still keep its developed country's position , such as US.

However, it may bring the question -Will Developing Countries ever catch up with Developed Countries? will remain unanswered because you have rightly pointed out that leaders of developing countries have given up on the economy and they keep themselves busy with other matters. Political institutions has great impact on the development of a nation. Industrial revolution happened in England instead of any other country because England had the best political institution that time. We have been hearing that if the 20th century belonged to developed countries of North America and Europe then 21st century will be of developing countries such as India, China and Brazil. But development is the crucial word which draws boundary between two countries-developed or developing. According to the World Bank reducing poverty is the main purpose of the development. After the World War 2, many nations have had significant growth however only few have been able to catch up with developed countries in terms of per capita income. From 1940s till 1990s poor countries grew slowly, falling farther behind to rich ones in income. Only few countries such as South Korea and Singapore were able to gain rich status. Since 2000, developing nations such as India and China are economically growing and managing growth rates of above 10% per year. With such continuous growth rates, developing nations can converge with developed nations and that would mean higher standard of living and good economic and political power. But this growth is limited to few countries since many countries still have not opened their domestic market to international markets. These countries also have barriers in technology and availability and allocation of resources. So, it seems that developing countries still need more time to develop exceed to the developed countries because they, such as China, Korea, Taiwan , Singapore etc. have poor technology and shortage of allocation or resource to compare the developed countries, such as US, UK etc. even their crime rate may reduce or many young people may accept to do the low skillful or low education level service jobs in societies.

● Developed countries lack effort to manufacture cheap products to sell strengths

Hence, we need to look at every economy as a company and developing a unique selling proposition becomes relevant. The United States has a USP of being the most technologically advanced and productive country. China has managed to become an exporter of cheap goods, the United Kingdom till now was a financial hub- there are chances of that changing thanks to BREXIT with the rise of Dublin. When we look at developing economies, such as India, we do not see any USP in the making. What is India's USP? I cannot think of any. People talk about demographic dividend to India in terms of a large young population. Such a population, which is largely uneducated is a demographic curse. Merely being a large market for goods and services is a bad idea for a USP. Developing countries need to introspect sometimes to look at the systemic challenges that they face. Looking towards developed economies is not always the best alternative. Such as China can choose to buy cheap product, because its technologic developement is poor. It is its strength to manufacture cheap products to sell to overseas to earn foreign income and raise GDP on export aspect. So, China may have much development chance to grow up its economy when it can decide which kinds of cheap or easier manufacturing products to sell to overseas when these countries can not supply from themselves manufactures, they need to buy from China in long time.

While the share of many western economies remained very low. However, over the years the trend started to reverse and many western countries have now become very developed while third world countries like India, China etc. continue on their journey from being developing to developed. We are currently a 2 trillion dollar economy and the eighth largest economy in the world. By 2030, India is predicted to be the fifth largest economy in the world. On purchasing power basis, India is the second largest economy in the world only behind China. Despite so many bright spots, we are faced with the paradox of being an advanced economy and still being one of the poorest in the world.

Otherwise, many such countries who are highly rich in natural resources continue to be plundered by the developed economies. Many countries continue to be haunted by the choices they made in past and turnaround being highly unlikely. They are often not helped by the injustices meted out by the developed economies who continue to take decision in their own self-interest. I feel the time has come when all the developing economies need to unite and raise their voice collectively. They need to speak about the unfair treatment meted out to them. A step in this regard has been taken by countries like India and China in important forums like UN and WTO. These breakout countries can act like role models and help create a more equitable world.

Another country is India, developing country , it may choose to manufacture and sell cheap products to any overeas countries to earn high GDP trade income. Till about 1750s, India was one of the largest economies in the world, contributing close to 25% of the world GDP. It was called the 'Golden Bird' and its products were world famed. The country has had huge trade surpluses for centuries through export of spices, finished cloth ('light woven air', it was called), and diamonds; all exotic products to that time period. It also had a thriving shipbuilding industry. There were accounts of Roman Establishments worrying about their riches syphoning off to India, because of the love of their woman towards Indian Cloth. India, thus essentially provided what the world desired & craved for, taking very few in return. This is despite the fact that it had one of the largest populations of that time. Then how come Indians achieve that richness and advancement, which seems difficult now? It is because, India was a hotbed of skilled people, who created exotic products, which were taken to the world by merchants in Indian built ships, which in turn were financed adequately by an established network of local people. So, although, India is not one high technologic development country, but it can choose what kinds of general cheap products to manufacture or catch any natural resources, e.g. growing up fishing industry, diamond industry. It is any one developed countries can not own strengths to compete to India easily.

Modern India and the ilk, are that they should spend more on Education and encourage Individual/SMEs (Small and Medium scale Enterprises), through adequate financing. The educational infrastructure should go to every nook and corner of the country like the 'temple complexes' providing accessible and affordable education, in the form of 'community colleges' in the US & 'skill enhancement centres'. Governments should support with adequate funds to create world-class universities of yesterday like 'The Nalanda', to provide cross-functional education and focus on innovation. The population should be encouraged to innovate & produce products, the world desires, like the 'light muslin cloth' or the 'iPhone' of the modern day, which shall bring huge trade surpluses. Industrialization should be decentralized through support for SMEs rather than purely going for High scale Industries. The financial infrastructure should be expanded enough to provide the financial support to every citizen, through banking services. Thus, on the whole, history can provide us with a lot of lessons on how to go about things, provided we have the interest to see from where we have come from. These lessons can be modified and applied to the current times, for we know these lands have done it before, for centuries. But, the only thing that requires here is 'Conviction' and if every country starts working on building these capacities, they becoming developed economies is just a matter of time!

● Climate change will impact developed countries to continue develop

Why does climate change impact developed countries to

continue develop more easily? It is one natural environment hurt problem , due to human,e.g. businessmen their damage our global natural environment behaviors, to cause any one developed countries may become developing countries in future one day in possible. I shal indicate the reasons as below:

The effects of climate change will not be uniformly distributed across the globe and there are likely to be winners and losers as the planet warms. Applying a broad brush to climate effects, developing countries are more likely to disproportionately experience the negative effects of global warming. Not only do many developing countries have naturally warmer climates than those in the developed world, they also rely more heavily on climate sensitive sectors such as agriculture, forestry and tourism. As temperatures rise further, regions such as Africa will face declining crop yields and will struggle to produce sufficient food for domestic consumption, whilst their major exports will likely fall in volume. This effect will be made worse for these regions if developed countries are able to offset the fall in agricultural output with new sources, potentially from their own domestic economies as their land becomes more suitable for growing crops. Moreover, developing countries may also be less likely to create drought resistant harvests given the lack of research funding.

Wild weather weighs on economies

The increased frequency and severity of extreme weather will weigh on government budgets. The aftermath of natural disasters often falls on authorities who are forced to spend vast amounts on clear-up operations and healthcare costs that come with experiencing extreme weather. Revenue reductions may also be experienced by countries heavily dependent on tourism or on selling fishing rights, fo

The effects on negative environment influence to developed countries and developing countries

As developed countries face an increasing strain on domestic budgets, fewer resources in the form of aid and economic development funds will flow to developing countries. The governments of these nations will be forced to channel resources away from productive and growth-enhancing projects towards countering the costs of extreme weather. Such effects will damage near-term growth prospects. Furthermore, developing countries are likely to have less capacity to rebuild. The time required to recover from natural disasters will be prolonged and if longer than the frequency in which such disasters occur, many developing economies could remain in a constant state of reconstruction.

Africa and Asia most at risk

Highly vulnerable regions in the emerging world include Sub-Saharan Africa and South and South East Asia, according to the World Bank. In South Asia, cities such as Kolkata and Mumbai will face increased flooding, warming temperatures and intense cyclones. Loss of snow melt from the Himalayas will also reduce the flow of water into the Indus Ganges and Brahmaputra basins. Meanwhile in South East Asia, Vietnam's Mekong Delta, which produces most of the rice, is especially vulnerable to rising sea levels. For Sub-Saharan Africa, food security will be a major challenge due to droughts and shifts in rainfall. Many developing nations are situated in low latitude countries and it is estimated that 80% of the damage from climate change may be concentrated. Consequently, higher agricultural yields, lower heating requirements and lower winter mortality rates are a handful of economic benefits climate change may bring, although these benefits may diminish as warming continues.

However, the prediction that developing countries will be disproportionately affected is reinforced by Standard and Poor's research on the influence climate change will have on sovereign risk. Recognising that climate change is a global mega-trend impacting sovereign risk through economic, fiscal and external performance, they find that lower-rated sovereigns appear most exposed. Based on these measures we can interpret the results in part as the susceptibility of an economy to climate change.

How poor climate change influences UK developed growth

In the UK, the average temperature is now 1°C higher that it was 100 years ago and 0.5°C higher than it was in the 1970s. As a higher latitude country, it is believed that the UK will fare better than many developing nations as global warming progresses. That is not to say the nation will escape the costs of climate change - particularly given its significant coastline where rising sea levels pose an obvious threat. According to scientists estimate of the cost of floods to the UK economy as a result of 3°C - 4°C of warming are in the region of 0.2% - 0.4% of GDP annually by the middle of the century, if flood management efforts are not strengthened.

In England, the south and parts of Yorkshire and Humberside are forecast to experience the greatest impact from flooding by 2050 . Aside from increased flooding, water availability will become progressively more constrained and droughts more frequent .Milder winters and the associated decline in cold-related mortality rates will be countered by a greater prevalence and severity of heat waves, bringing with it a higher number of heat-related mortalities. Finally, with the agricultural sector contributing approximately just 0.6% of GDP, the benefits of longer growing seasons will be marginal to the economy.

In conclusion, climate change may also indirectly affect the UK economy through global supply chains. The UK may both export to and import from climate-sensitive countries. The subsequent influence of climate change in these economies may feed through to the domestic economy through lower demand for exports or higher prices of imports.

V

Factors Influence Human Future High Technological Development Failure

Why do developed countries need to improve on culture, education, medical technologyl development aspects?

I shall attempt to explain that why America, Japan, England and India these four countries ought need to improve on above sevearal aspects as below:

Firstly, I shall explain that why Japan still needs to improve itself country technology development, although Japan had been a technological mature development country in long time. In Japan technological development history, Japan had owned high technological development on technological products manufacture aspect, such as electronic rice cookers, artificial intelligent rice cookers cars, televisions etcl technological products. But when Germany had also began to develop high technological products in global technological prodict market. In basic, all any similar Japan technological products. Germany had also owned high technological skills to manufacture to sell in global high technological products marekt.

So, nowadays, Germany may still be Japan's high technological product main competitor. It means that global homeholders technology products consumers, car buyers must choose any Germany and Japan high technological products to compare which are better quality in order to satisfy their useful need.s Hence, in global high technological products market, Japan won't be still high technological product leader as past history. If Japan did not continue to improve its technology, Germany will be the future high technology product leader to replace Japan, hence Japan can not neglect to consider how to continue to improve its technology development.

IN the past, science and technology in Japan is focused in vehicle manufacture technology, consumer electronic, robotics, medical devices, space exploration and film industry. For example, Japan's focus on intensive mathematics education and the reverence for engineers in Japanese culture aids enginnering talent development which as produced advances in automative engines, television display technology, videogames , optical clocks etc. On aerospace exploration aspect Japan had conducted space and planetary research., aviation research and development of space and satellites. On nuclear power development technology, since 1973, Japan has been looking to become less dependent on imported fuel and start on depend on nuclear energy. On electronic development aspect, Japan is well known for its electronic industry throughout the world, and Japanese electronic products account ofr a large share in the world market. However, Japan had beed a leading nation in scientific research, particularly biomedical research.

However, all of above technology, Germany will own advance technology to replace Japan to develop its products to sell to global easily. Germany had innovated its technology, e.g. the self -driving cars of the near future depend on precise digital geolocation data to navigate to arrive at destinations. So, Germany's non-manual driving vehicles innovation may be future nay countries car users' suppliers. Also, its battery technology is also one of future high technology mission 2021. Germany government began to support the construction of autonomous capacities in battery cell production to secure technological maximally exploit the battery calue chain. Germany government should continue to support electronic battery cell manufacturers, to drive force in the growing market for electronic cars and the goals of continuing to build their motors in Germany in the future.

Is Germany technology advanced? I believe that it is true, in the index's eighth edition for 2020, Germany was named the most technologically advanced nation, followed by South Korea, and Singapore, Germany is most known for its engineering, different high technological invention etc. aspect. Why is Germany so technologically advanced? Because Germany had been an academic powerhouse for a long time and as such education is focused on technological aspect. It's education goal is for good ideas to be translated quickly into innovative products and services. Moreover, Germany also considers Hyper automation, the distributed cloud, technological development. Some technological leaders predict the future high technological development countries may include: China, South Korea, United States , Singapre , United Kingdom, Russia, Japan and Germany .

The possible number or rank technological development countries rank may be 1 South Korea rank 2 ,ay be United States, rank 3 may be Japan, rank 4 may be Sweden nowadays. However, Germany may be future rank 1 technological leader, because Germany is so good at engineering. Germany's engineers borne out of the country are world leaders in their field, reowned for their dedication to precision, function and power. Over the years, Germany engineers have maintained their reputation to help Germany technology development products to as a top exporter of machinery and industrial equipment.

Moreover, in human development history, Germany are smart, when Germans are the most intelligent people in Europe, the British have an edge over rivals in France when it comes to the grwy matter , a new league of IQ scores has shown. The scored 94 and Germans were tap of the table with an IQ of 107, according to Richard Lynn, who headed the study. However, why is German technology will be the best. The major factor for Germany's success is that it has managed to homegrown scientific research and expertise to move up the technological ladder, concentrating on innovative products and processes not easily copied or undercut by cheap wages. The textile industry is a case in point, hence it causes that future Germany's technology development may be Japan's future one main competitos in technological product development market. So, it is right time, Japan needs to continue to research its new technological invention in order to improve its technological development to be the best to compare other high technological development countries.

Secondly, I shall discuss that why US needs to improve or change itself country's culture to let many different countries people can adopt to live. For example, nowadays, COVID 19 illness is serious to influence any one country people live. IN fact, US ia a developed country, it is global countries only one leader to encourage different countries people to live. Also, US is one comfortable living people to let global immigrants to feel. But, when COVID 19 disease occurred, some US people feel that it is possible due to Chinese people , they contact COVID 19 disease to cause many US people get this kind of disease. However, it is none evidence to prove this kind of illness may be caused by Chiese to cause many US people die. So, US, opening culture began to change worse, e.g. some US people began to hate overseas immigrants to live itself country, it is possible due to many US people feel afraid to contact overseas immigrants, they may bring COVID 19 disease in their bodies, so when US people they contact these overseas COVID 19 disease immigrants, they may get this kind of disease . SO, it seems that US people's opening accept to let overseas immigrant living policy has changed to prohibit them to immigrate to live US easily.

However, I feel that US 's closing culture mind can not bring its social development to improve more easily. US ought to change its social culture has more opening cultural mind as before how it accepted different countries immigrants to choose US to live. Hence, it brings this question: What challenges US may encounter if it can be change its new cultural mind to accept more overseas immigrants to live easily? The challenges may include: American needs to understand themselves value and learn about what is important to Americans know why Americans value independence, equality and being on time. Americans will need see they are direct and informal and why competition, work ethic, and buying things are important in the US. American probably had strong traditions and culture that they valued. In the UNited States, there are also important American values are the things that are most important to Americans. For example, one of the main American values is independence. Independence is sometimes referred to US individualism. Americans are very proud of being self reliant, or being able to take care of themselves. American children tend to leave the home earlier than in oterh cultures, if they continue to live at home, they might be asked to pay rent or contribute to the house. So, Americans expect anyone who is able to work to do in order to support themselves. Also, Americans value privacy and their own space, when in some cultures wanting privacy may be seen as a bad thing, many Americans like to have alone time and may be private abour certain topic. In conversations, many Americans are private about certain things and do not want to talk about them, such as age, how much money they make, or their political, sexual and religious views. Americans often give each other more space in public situations than people in other cultures . They tend to stand with a bit of space between them, typically the distance of direct. This means that they often tell you what they think and they will be assertive about when they want.

Some peoples of American-style directness,, such as in conversation, if an American disagrees with youropinion, they might tell you, this does not mean they do not like you, just that they may have a different area. In classes, Americans may challenge their teachers' ideas. IN some culture, it is impolite to disagree with your teacher, it is never is rude to ask for help. Most Americans love to help and need very little encouragement to become good friends and neighbors.

However, I feel that America has lose equality value. Although, many newly immigrants moved to America to follow American team. They believed that if you worked hard, you could move up in society. But, today, more and more people realize the American dream is not true. Many people who work very hard do not have very much money. Often people who love from privileged backgrounds have an easier time moving up in the world. Still, the idea of equality is an important part of US culture.

So, COVID 19 disease occurrence had explained that US began have inequality culture difference causes, discrimination to overseas immigrants, e.g. Chinese. Americans discrimination behavior began to cause. American ought change itself new culture to traditional culture to accept different countires clever immigrants skills, talent people mind in order to help itself country to continue develop more advanced society to be world leader position.

Thirdly, I shall discuess why England needs to improve education. What negative impacts will happen, if UK does not continur improve education as well as its neglect on improvement education, how it will bring negative impact to its studetns minds in society? Why growth is the key to improve UK education development? Conventional wisdom states that smaller schools provide students with a better education . But studies of education systems around the world, show that growing schools could actually solve UK's poor student outcomes.

Nowadays, the UK's school system is in trouble, despite the fact that the last two decades have seen massive changes in the UK's education sector. UK education report indicated that in the past 15 years, the UK's four countries have spent $550 UK billion on operating and enhancing their secondary schools. IN the same period, England alone closed 35% of its schools (1,500 institutions) and opened almost 2,000 new ones . Nonetheless, little has improved UK education report indicated that in 2026, only 65% of all English pupils graduated with five or more grade as compared with 50% 15 years ago, at a cost od $37 billion per percentage point of improvement. The US was as a wholw spent the 8 th largest amount of 34 OECD countries, but only came, 19 th in mathemactics, 16 th in reading and 14 th in science.

So, what 's going wrong to cause UK students have worse learning performance. The reasons may include: Neglecting all four nations education reforming. Education in the UK is devolved to the four nations that make up the British union. For this reason, most of qualifications data relates only to England, although total spending figures are mostly UK wide. Academy shcools are amodel of schooling that is available only in England. There is no provision for the model in the other three nations of the UK.

The next reason is failure educational strategy. UK education report also indicated that England's strategy over the past 15 years has been to try to improve its education system by fixing its low lights , less than a third of students graduate with five or more GCE grade , reducing their projected lifetime earnings by $140,000. By putting their schools into " special measures" and offering them up for tender to other schools, it hopes that whole education system would improve. BUt, it has not . THe English have thrown more money at the proble,, spending 84% more on each child's education . Then, they did 15 years ago ($57,000 rather than $31,000), but although half their schools have improved, the other half have declined, and the overall picture is still the same. So, there are still many UK schools can not get UK government help to improve all school students individual learning effort to be better.

● What would have happened if UK government had spent the last 15 years trying to grow their education system bright lights, rather than brighten , their low lights?
UK education improvement strategy is such that a similar change in strategy helped the charity save the children reduce malutrition by 80% in Vietnam over two years, after decades of getting. Instead of trying to solve the poor learning ability of student learning performing problems in their worst areas, UK educators also need to expand a similar improvement education on strategy shift in order to help transform to UK any schools reforming educational policies in success.
Hence, if England had adopted another long term countrywide educational strategy, where all schools work together to improve standards across the UK in order to access all schoools resources, facilities and entracurricular activities and it could shown that good teachers in both schools can teach anyone. Then, most of UK teachers can know their subject inside out and quickly adapt their teaching methods to different needs. Consequently, when UK can imporve most of UK students learning effort to the best performance, as better educated students are more knowledgeable, money when they can attribute their the best effort to their society in the future. Then, UK society can be developed to reach the most top level, because UK's future development must depend on its next generation's help. If future UK education can train many talent students to attribute to social different aspects, such as technology,

medical , business, construction etc. different professional aspects . UK future social development may be improved to be better to compare present society development. So, UK government can not neglect how to improve all UK student individual learning performance in order to help every UK student to pursue their abilities to prepare to attribute to UK future society devleopment successfully.

Finally, I shall discuss why India will need to improve medical technology. Recently, world news reported that INdia has many people are killed by COVID 19 disease. India is the highest population country. I assume that COVID 19 disease causes many Indians die because India has no enough hospitals, clinics to provide good medical quality to serve these COVID 19 disease contact patients. Due to lack of the best medical skillful doctors and nurses. So, many COVID 19 disease patients can not be saved to their lifes, even in India society, many none of COVID 19 disease contact people, when they contact to the COVID 19 disease people, they can not give good drugs to save themselves lifes. SO, it explains why India has many people are killed by COVID 19 disease in short time . SO, it seems that India lacks enough drugs to supply to these COVID 19 disease patients to cause there are many COVID 19 disease patients die in short time.

This COVID 19 diease attracks India matter occurs, it brings these questions: IS short time shortage of drug supply factor or long time shortage of drug supply factor to cause many COVID 19 disease patients die? Can long time poor medical technology factor cause many Indians die? IS COVID 29 disease the main factor causes many Indians die? India has many people are living. So, India must eed to improve its medical technology in order to solve the number increasing of India people future health challenge.

One of the most important and highly debated, elements of India society is the quality of healthcare available to patients. The use of technology increases provider capability and patient access when improving the quality of life for some India clients and saving the lives of others. The India technology role can play in improving health of India. It can help in early detection of health problems. It cn also help in data collected from tests instantly monitor, the conditon of the patient, and then relay that information to the doctors and staff of the overall healthcare system.

However, the factors have made improvement in health conditions possible in India , they may include: A downtrend in communicable diseases, a focus on prevention , reduced neonatal mortality rates, tacking antimicrobial resistance, improved nutrition, using digital health and artificial intelligence for social impact, stronger government accountability. A number of industry analysts have observed that increased accessibility of treatment is one of the most tangible ways that technology has changed healthcase. Health IT opens up may more avenues of exploration and research, which allows experts make helathcare more driven and effectve than it has ever been. Hence, future India may apply these new medical technology, e.g. virtual reality, precision medicine, health wearables, artificial organs, 3D printing, wireless brain sensors, robotic surgery, smart inhalers, they are the main treatment option for asthma and if taken correctly, will be effective for 80% of India patients.

Hence, India must need solve medical technology improvement challenge in order to keep many people lifes , in special for the talent youngers, e.g. doctors, scientists, architects, lawyers, accountants , atc. professionals. I believe that India's medical technology can not been improved to raise quality in order to save many COVID 19 disease patents their lifes. So, many of COVID 19 disease patients can not been saved by good quality if medical drugs in short time. So, if INdia does not hope to lose many young talent professionals, it must need to continue improve its medical technology as soon as possible.

● How can our future social development can be improved ?

Nowadays, globalization cooperation or our societies become one society to any countries leaders is needed. I believe that countries competition will be serious, even we shall attack other countries if any one country can not accept " globalization cooperation mind". I mean that it is only globalization cooperation one way choice, then our societies can be improved or will be become better more easily.

For China and America two countries example, recently, because COVID 19 disease caused many Western and Asia countries began feel that COVID 19 disease was caused from Chinese. However, they have no evidence to indicate that COVID 19 disease must be caused from China. Although, before the year end of two years, there are some Chinese had ever travelers to US, then US had many people began to get this kind COVID 19 disease to cause many American die, when they did not believe that COVID 19 disease can cause human dies easily. Until to now, global many people had gotten this kind of illness to vause they die, when the health person contacts the owned COIVD 19 disease sick people . Although some people can be saved after they are saved by drug, but many people can not be saved, when they can not been saved by drug, even they still can not saved after they had been gotten drug. Such as US, UK, India, China,

Germany , Korea, Japan, France these countries reported that they had many people could not saved to keep their lifes when they could not believe that they can get COVID 19 disease when they contact to the strange people who may owned COVID 19 diesease easily, when they are sitting down to the same table to eat in restaurants or when the COVID 19 disease strange person and the health person are talking together closely.

So, I believe that it is right time to any countries leaders need to act and to cooperate to find the method to avoid COVID 19 disease attacks any people. I mean the globalization cooperation attitude may nee to ourselves countries leaders . Our country leader can not only consider himself/herself country benefit and neglact to consider other countries benefits. If global humans hope that we can still to improve our culture to be peace or improve our space technology artificial intelligent development manufacturing to the advance level rapidly, or improve our medical technology to the best quality or improve our students learning effort or teachers teaching performance to reach the most satisfactory need to our future any one students. It is only global cooperation way to achieve global improved societies aim. If our societies or any one country leader still only consider how to protect himself/herself country businessmen benefits and leader himself/herself benefits, and rich people benefits , but they neglect to consider any one citizen benefits ,e.g. the low education, poor old age people, low income people in societies.Then, unfair and discrimination will be encouraged to occur in any one country society . Consequently when any one country low education , low income , poor old people can not feel comfortable to lieve in themselves countries. They will feel angry to complain themselves countries governments and leader individual ambitious behavior to influence these group people feel unhappy to live long time in themselves countries.

Consequently, the country's social education level will only continue to worse, even economy will continue recession, as ell as and kind of technologies won't continue improve. Due to our future any one country leader can not keep globalization cooperation mind or positive opening attitude to let any one itself country citizen feels comfortable to live forever. Then, the developed country ,e g. US, UK will not still keep technology development leading position easily. It is possible due to they only consider themselves social benefits, during this COVID 19 disease had been attacking themselves countries. So, they ought also consider other countries , they are attacked by COVID 19 disease, hoe to avoid COVID 19 disease will continue to attack any one country easily.

Hence, we only cooperate to help ourselves to find the best long time method to fight COVID 19 disease . When our countries leaders can cooperate to spend time to sit down to discuss how to fight COVID 19 disease , then I believe that our global societies may been improved more better rapidly as soon as possible in this year.

● Methods to avoid future human developmend failure

Finally, I shall conclude that how we can avoid human development failure. we need to know that human is facing threat of self-benefit behavior. We can follow our development to analyze why we shall encounter failure of improvement stage in our soon future. In our past thousand years, human had developed in success from fishing, agriculture stage till to manufacture industry innovation stage, till to nowadays high technological development stage ,even our future artificial intelligent high technology

(non-manual control machine stage). Although all of our past development , till to nowadays development, it seems that we can develop in success in any technological aspects ,e.g. space, computer , internet , ecommerce , medical technology etc. even future non-manual control (AI) artificial intelligent technology. But, some ways may help us to continue high technological development in success, even damage our future continue high technological development. They may include unfriend or poor culture development, lacking globalization cooperation, self -beefit mind factors.

All of above factors are any countries leades self-benefit mind or negative attitude (human behavior) to influence our future high technology continue development can succeed in possible. The reason is because that if any one country leader only considers how to protect himself/ herself country technological development beefit, it means that he/she does not allow his/her country talent scientists can discess their any new technological invention opinions to let other countries talent scientists to learn ho to improve themselves new technological invention together. This point is the main bad factor to cause human future any kinds of high technological development to delay in possible, because our any kinds of high technological development success, we must depend on global scientists can have chance to share their any kinds of new technological experiments to let they can learn why the scientist can develop the kind of product in success, or why the scientist can not develop the kind of product in success. Then, any one country scientists can absorb other countries scientists their successful or failure scientific experiements in order to improve their any kinds of new technological expeiment to achieve the most satisfactory scientific experiement demand to bring benefit to us. So, globalization cooperation is the only way to avoid human development failure absolutely.

● Why do developed countries need to continue to learn how to improve new technology ?

In fact, there are different between developing and developed countries. Developing countries, such as Afria, Korea, China, Taiwan, these countries are developing, so their IT information , medical, manufacturing technology, artificial intelligence etc. different industries are not mature, they must need to continue improvement to develop their skills in order to satisfy consumers market need. Because social need had been often changing, so these developing countries scientists, businessmen need to have good learning mind to prepare to learn how technological , medical , artificial intelligent, IT knowledge in order to satisfy consumer individual new product useful need and keep market competitive effort in themselves home an overseas consumption markets both more easilu. But, why do developed countries also need to continue to learn how to improve new technology? What negative impacts will bring to developed countries their scientists and businessmen do not continue to improve their new products development or continue to research how to improve their old products to achieve the best quality to order consumers needs.

Nowadays, global consumption market competition is serious. Consumer individual need or demand is increasing, when one consumer feels the kind of old product can not satisfy his/her actual need, he/she will seek to find which brands of products, they have similar function or useful characteristics in order to make comparison to other similar kinds of products. Then, he/she will make final purchase decision. So, when the consumer had habit to use the brand of product, it does not mean that he/she will continue to use this brand of product. He/she may be influenced to change to choose the another brand of similar function characteristics of new product to buy use in this rapid changing competitive market.

Hence, if the developed country's culture is changed to closing mind from opening mind. These developed country, such as US people can not accept to other countries people new, useful, attributing innovativ mind of ideas easily. They only consider or recognite that themselves ideas are the best or the most useful. Consequently, due to their foolish closing minds, their traditional protection themselves believes will cause difficult to continue to improve or develop, because it is possible that there are any other developed countries, e.g. UK, Germany, Japan, they have some talent people, scientists their technological skills may be proficient or more advanced to compare US, itself countries some scientists.

So, I recommend that any developed countries can not only consider to appreciate themselves countries scientists must be the most smart to compare other developed countries. Any one developed country scientists ought need to cooperate with other developed countries scientists to discuss or research any new invention together in order to help themselves technology can been improved rapidly in order invent many different kinds of new products to satisfy consumers themselves often changing useful needs in this global consumption market nowadays.

This developed country Japn is one good example to explain that why its scientists ought need to continue to improve their different technology or science skills as well as learn any new kinds of technology or science knowledge from other developed countries scientists , such as US, UK, Germany together. Because it is only one effective technology and science improvement method (way) to Japan scientists,when they can accept the other developed scientists different new or innovated opinions as well as they can spend some time to sit down to discuss and cooperate to help themselves old products how to change or innovate new products in order to attract global consumers purchase choice. So, although, Japan had been one developed country long time, its technology development had searched mature stage in the past, But, it can not reprsent that its technology must be more advanced to compare other developed countries, such as UK, US, Germany. Because these any one developed country, their scientists still continue carry on researching how to improve themselves old products to be new. So, it seems that Japan's any old technological products, e.g. smart phones, television, washing machines, rice coolers, products won't bring more attract to persuade global consumers choices. Because US, UK, Germany etc. different developed countries scientists had began to research how to continue improve its traditional old technological products to be more attraction in order to adopt global technological products users needs. For example, developing country India, due to its medical technology is poot, if it hopes to improve itself country technology, it must need to attempt to concentrate on spending money, medical teaching resources on medical technology aspect. India's medical technology improvement must be any kinds of technologies , the most need to improve to compare IT technology, manufacturing technology, artificial intelligent technology, space technology etc. The reason is that India is the highest population country, if its medical technology's cost, it will cause many young talent people die, such as COVID 19 disease occurs to India recently. It causes many Young talent Indians die, due to it lasks enough good medical technology to supply drugs to save them. So, if India government hopes that it can have many talent high skillful technology youngers to serve itself country. It will need to consider how to improve its medical technology in order to fight any possible new kind of illness attack, instead of COVID 19 disease, when India can improve its medical technology to save many young talent scientists' lifes . Then, it won't lose many talent scientists and they can continue to attribute themselves scientific knowledge for India itself country lont time technological science development.

Hence, UK and US both governments need to consider how to allocate enough land to supply to any manufacturing and business operations efficiently, how to help any educational organizations to train talent employees and school organizations to teach talent students, how to supply enough loan to assist any business founders to develop their new businesses in success or create new entrepreneurship. All of these can bring advantages to satisfy their societies needs.

Economists generally agree that highly economic development and growth are influenced by four factors: Human resources, physical capital, natural resource and technology. So, in general, US an UK countries hope they can become highly developed countries have government that focus on these areas. They mean that factors may influence one developed country to continue to become highly developed country, factors may include: accumulation of capital stock, increases in talent labor inputs, such as workers or hour worked, technological advancement. All of these factors may assist UK , US continue to bring highly development benefit. So, UK, US are such as industrialization in developed countries, they need to improve these industrial productivity in order to continue to keep, highly developed countries in possible, these factors may include: long term technological development, improvement quality of human resources, encough availability of finace, efficient managerial talent, efficient government policy and surplus of enough supply of natural factor, e.g. good climate for agriculture, enough natural coal , land natural resource supply. However, they also need to consider these are negative factors to affect them to continue develop, e.g. lack of drive of social motivation for improvement, unproductive social functions, such as war or having very large family sizes, negative social cultures, such as gambling and drinking wine, and lack of skills due to poor training and education . They may be poor social negative factors to influence they continue develop in success.

VI

Future Human Transport Need Change How To Improve Developing And Developed countries Social transport System

What the psychological need differences between rail and bus passengers

● Reasons we need to improve public bus transport tool service quality

The ways that we need to improve public transport, e.g. bus transport service, we try our best to ask these questions: During periods of stress on the bus, like weather conditions or maintenance failure that slows the bus service system? How to improve mass transit on bus service frequency, when looking at ways to improve public bus service transport , riders want frequency? Interestingly, speed is not as much of an issue, if they are waiting downtown in the rain, or on some suburban backstreet, riders want to know that a bus will arrive soon, preferably in less than 15 minutes. Therefore, the wait becomes part of the transportation cycle. Even, if the bus is lightning fast, in the mind of the rider, the trip begins right when they arrive at the bus station, and start waiting for the bus to pick them up.

`

`What does efficient bus ticketing system mean? It is big part of how to improve bus transportation efficiency is improving transit ticketing system, because ticketing systems have to be quick and practical to allow for prompt loading and unloading of passengers. So, inefficient ticketing systems also slow down bus frequency, as drivers need to wait for everyone to tap before they can drive away to the next stop.

How to let passengers feel comfortable? Riders want comfortable buses that can seat as many people as possible. Face-to-face seating is not appealing and being knee-to-knee in a confined space creates awkward moments between strangers. However, comfort also extends beyond the buses' seating arrangements. A smooth riding, quiet bus plays a significant role in reducing the overall stress of a public transit experience. Among the consistent feedback from riders of fuel cell electric buses is a surprised delight about how quiet the buses are when in motion.

On reduce greenhouse gases environment prote3ctoin aspect, exhaust spewing buses are on ongoing concern. One of the significant factors that commuters consider when deciding to take public transit is the environment impact of their alternative transport method. And although a diesel bus packed with 40 people may be less environmentally damaging than 40 separate diesel cars, it will still have negative impacts on both local air quality and the overall climate situation , when given the choice, we've found nearly all riders prefer " zero-emission buses" to conventional diesel buses nowadays.

IN fact, we are always thinking of ways to improve public transportation by dev4eloping new clean fuel technologies. Fuel cell electric buses resolve some of the above issues for both transit bus operators, bus performance is continually being proven and improved over millions of miles of operation in environments ranging from mountain villages to desert communities to busy cities. Hence, the first step to creating better public transit networks is becoming aware of the available options. Many communities are taking measures to improve public transport by implementing innovative sustainable transport solutions that have profound impacts on the live ability of their communities.

So, I shall recommend these ways to improve public transport methods to bus service as below:

Firstly, making interchanging easy for public transport has most efficient public transport service improvement aim at linking areas that are outside a city to the city center., doing this is beneficial in two ways. It helps people who should not at the city center , but needed to pass through because the outlying areas are not connected together to keep off and hence reduce congestion at the center. Also, connecting the outlying areas provide a backup for the public transport system in case of a problem which often happen.

Secondly, minimize the number of stops/ stations, stops and stations improve the efficiency of public transport , but there should be a balance between enabling accessibility with more steps or stations and reducing the costs of operation by increasing transit need of ensure trips are covered in time. Therefore, core should be taken to ensure that stops and stations are located on streets to balance accessibility by commuters on one hand and reduces operating cost on the other hand.

Thirdly, lessen traffic congestion by deploying a number measures. Reducing traffic congestion at city streets could be done, implementing a number of strategies, such as providing lanes dedicated specially for the use of public transport, deploying strict regulations , such as queue bypasses or queue jumps. Another means of reducing traffic congestion is by providing feeds and data from public transport systems, freely to commuters to educate and help them avoid areas of traffic congestion and finally, giving priority to public and trams operating efficiency, increasing the travel time of these engineering mechanism whereby a traffic signal turns green at the light of a public transport at an intersection. All of above these improvements may be future public transport bus passengers service improvement need, if any bus companies hope to increase their bus passengers number absolutely.

● What rail passengers really want rail innovation improvement

Public transport systems, such as rail provides benefits including less traffic congestion, less pollution, safe travels, lower expenditures , less effort and better predictability in comparison to road transport. In fact, bus and train riders experience the most negative emotions in comparison with other transport modes, such as private cars , walking and cycling. Hence, technology has the potential to bring about the changes, needed to increase efficiency of rail transport, e.g. cost-effective ways to improve the quality of public transport and increase ridership may involve comfort and convenience improvement, or technology has the potential to provide more up-to-date information and customized service to train passengers and therefore improve the rail journey experience . On the overall, passenger journey , e.g. the importance of automated traveller information systems, and electronic fare payment collection systems can bring rail passengers look for this information in different interfaces from localized displays installed on platforms to smartphone applications.

Moreover, technology can also improve fare collection and management which of made manually can be prone to error, and time consuming , unified cards, smartphones can make it easier for rail passengers to obtain ticket, with the potential to increase the user satisfaction with the rail system. Because rail passengers demand not only pre-trip information for planning their travels, but also information during journeys, such as punctuality, connections and platform allocation. One extensive review indicates that accurate communication, for example, giving effective way finding information, can optimize passengers' experience with public transport.

Also, technology can facilitate the process of finding free seats on trains, which is a current demand from rail passengers and the cause of stress during the boarding process. IN fact, many rail passengers have specific preferences regarding seats and would appreciate having control of where to sit. So, navigation and way finding information can be delivered directly to passengers to inform where they could stand aiming to board less busy carriages, for example, choosing to travel on a less crowded train, or spreading themselves out on the platform before boarding in respond to crowding information, e.g. smartphones are frequently used by passengers of public transport and can make waiting times seem shorter. Furthermore specific system features designed for train passengers have the potential to improve the journey experience of the travelling public.

What ferry passengers service improvement need

● How can ferry service be improved affordable, reliable, convenient, flexible and clean will get drivers out of their cars ad onto environmentally responsible to passenger ferries?

Ferry transportation provides an environmentally friendly commuting alternative to the congested roadways in many of countries , so ferry transport service needs to meet long term air quality goals, it is critical to move beyond traditional technologies to zero-and near zero emissions technology. Clearly putting a transit system in operation that demonstrates emission control technology and the development of zero-emissions, ferries will help achieve air quality goals to our societies, for example., new shipping rout4es are needed to increase in order to satisfy ferry passengers different rapid ferry journey short distance need, when they need to choose one kind of public transport service either bus or rail or ferry transport service among of them.

None ferry accident occurrence, ferry service needs to let passengers to feel it is the safest sea pubic transit, expanded recreational service is also needs, particularly on weekends when bridge , corridor traffic congestion is becoming an increasing problem. Ferry service needs have uniquely provided flexible, vital transportation supports in response to a natural or man-made disaster that shuts down bridges and roads, fuel –cell technology is needed , that will lead to zero-emissions ferries, e.g. on-board emissions monitoring is far less polluting than previously through, e.g. 149 passenger boats are designed to travel 25 knots or less , and 300-350 passenger vessels designed for speeds up to 30-35 knots.

This emissions standard will perform specifications and the cost of this technology is accounted for in the ferry company vessel capital budget ,e.g. vessel design capabilities to accommodate existing and new docking configurations . This maximizes fast ferry passenger loading, including bicycles, carriages and wheelchairs. Hence, future global ferry service needs have these positive influence to our societies: Need for flexibility, desire to help the environment, need for time saving, which includes the importance of reliability, sensitivity to personal travel experience, such as a need for personal space or quiet feeling ferry seat any time, insensitivity to transport cost, e.g. the ferry ticket price is cheaper than rail or bus fares sensitivity to stress.

However, ferry service is different unlike rail, bus because expanded ferry service can be launched quickly at low initial cost and with great flexibility. Unlike buses, ferries are not hindered by traffic congestion on roads and highways or in tunnels. So, ferry service can be safely expanded to bring new service to new places and add more service to existing routes more easily than bus and rail public transport both, e.g. expanded ferry transport service can operate safety and provide with a robust, flexible and effective emergency response capability if the region is hit with a natural or man-made event that disables roads, other transit, bridges , before any.

Hence, ferry companies need to decide to improve their ferry transport service, they need to answer these questions: Is the new shipping route a good transportation investment? Does the new shipping route have fatal environmental negative impact? Does it offer a transit option that can be initiated in a timely and cost-effective manner? Can it provide ferry transport service that is reliable, safe and fully accessible after the ferry recovery would be unreasonably high charge to ferry selection is decided to implement to increase?

Also, ferry safety is needed to consider because it can influence any ferry passenger choice, when the ferry is moving on the sea, when the passenger is sitting on the boat. The ferry safety issue may include: Ensuring that access to all ferry operational areas, including, machinery spaces, pilothouse and gear lockers, remain locked at all times and accessible only to authorized crew, posting night watch security guards at terminals, conducting diligent onboard inspection for unattended passenger bags, briefcases and packages after each run, before the next boat load is allowed to board, creating coded signals and response to report suspicious activity, requiring positive identification before allowing any contractors, vendors or others access to ferries, providing additional security training to crew, developing a security plan to account for potential threats, outlining preventive measures and detailing an action plan in the event of a threat or actual emergency.

Future Human Transport Need Change

How future our transport need change? What factors influence our future transport need change? In general, these factors may influence our transportation need change. They may include fuel cost, the labor market for commercial drivers, demand for frieight , customer loyalty , vehicle capacity, government regulation, geographical events, the public transport tool reputation to passegners as a merchant. However, the factors that influence the development of transport system in an area? They may include as below:

Environment at the local scale existing hydrographical and geomorphological characteristics are string, factors in transport development, particularly in terms of the technical challenges (bridge, gradients,) they present to construct, other factors may include historical, technological, political and economic factors. All of these factors may influence our future transport system how develops. For raiway development influential factors, they may include: Geograohical factors, e.g. the North Indian plain with its level land, high density of population and rich agriculture presents the most favourable conditions for the development of railways in India. However, the presence of large number of rivers makes it necessary to construct bridges which involve heavy expenditure to Indian Government publich transport expenditure.

How transport has changed from past to present?

There has been a remarkable development in modern transportation. The stream engine and then the stream trains have emerged and spread at this time and in abundance until the discovery of natural gas and oil was an evolution of transportation. Thus, the sedams and vehicles began to run in oil, until present battery changes energy vehicle need, even future non-manual driving artificial intelligent driving vehicle need. These new transport technology may influence our future public transportation from gas energy to battery changed energy, even non-manual driving vehicles need to our daily transport need.

So, our future purpose of public transport need is the unique purpose to oversome space, which is shaped by a variety of human and physical constraints, such as distance, time. These both is our future main public transport need main purpose factors, short distance and reducing journey time, they influence that why we need to choose to catch any kinds of public transportation tool to replace purchase private cars to drive transport tool choice. So, future any kinds of public transport tools, they need to consider above both main factors , how to attract passengers to choose to catch themselves public transport tools choice in this competitive public transport tools market.

On the other hand, the economic importance of transportation development can be defined as improving the welfare of a society, through appropriate social, political and economic conditions , such as US Government spent too much money to assist MTR (MAss transport railway firm) to develop underground thrain transport. Its aim to let many passegner can reduce journey time and reduce distance between destinations, it also hopes US citizen passengers can pay cheap transport fare to buy ticket to catch underground transport train for many families their transport expenditure in social transport welfare view.

However, US Government neds to solve those challenges, before it implements to develop rapid underground railway , e.g. lack of knowledge of geographical fwatures, lack of manpower necessary to operate the rapid underground railway construction work, lack of construction materials within the US itself. For Brazil rail network transportation development example, the factors influence the use of rail network for transportion is highly restricted in Brazil. Thus, the development of roadways and waterways is the main modes of transportation that caould be used in Brazil given its topography and drainage benefit to society . So, brazil can develop rail network for transportation development in success.

So, transportation system is important in the development of any nation, because transportation plays important role in rapid economic growth of a nation. Thrapsortation increases the quality and variety of consumer goods, thereby stimulating the demand and development of trade and economy of the nation. Moreover, transport provides various employment opportunities and boosts up the economy of the country.

Also, any transport tools need to improve themselves transport service in order to attract passengers to choose their public transport service more easily. They may attempt to sign up for an autonomous vehicle pilot program, free phone enquiey concerns whether the passegner can catch which bus bumber to go to the destination, hou much bus fare, how long journey time, when the bus will arrive teh bus stops or leave the bus stop etc. bus service questions, before any one passenger prepares to choose to catch bus (free bus go phone call enquiry), free download a public transport tool transit app. even water taxi tranport tool innovation can replace ferry public transport tool, it can let passengers have more fun an enjoyable catching feeling. So, water taxi tranport tool is one kind of future new transport tool change to replace ferry , it can influence ferry passengers to choose water taxi public transport tool to replace ferry. Although, its fare may be more expsnse to compare ferry, but it can reduce jounrey time and distance between both water stations, when ferry can not arrive the other destinations, but water taxi can arrive any one water station destination. It can bring convenient to future any one ferry passengers. So, water taxi may be developed to some countries, e.g. New Zealand , Auckland city, US , Washington and New York cities they had developed water taxi public transport tools to let ferry passengers have one kind new water public transport choice.

However, instead of new transport innovation improvement to water transport service public transport with input from the public on bus transport service aspect, bus frequency improvement, it means when booking at ways to improve, bus frequency from long times to less times, efficient bus ticketing system, a big part of how to improve tranportation efficiency is improving transit ticketing system.

In fact, my future transport system may still include these five types, modes of transport are: railway, roadways, airways, waterways and piplelines. Also, among different includes of transport, railways are the different modes of transport, railways are the cheapest. Trains cover the distance in less time and comparatively, the fare is also less to other modes of transporation. Therefore, railways is the cheapest mode of transportation to compare ferry, water taxi , sea transport, bus, taxi, road system.

On conclusion, transport price is not the main factor to attract passegners to choose to catch. The importance to have a good public transport system in place. It may be one main factor to help the kind of public transport tool to attract passengers to choose to catch, because a good transport links can widen people's job search area and help them find employment. It can also reduce commuting times and reduce the cost of living, and high skilled workers are more likely to travel across longer distances to work, especially if they are following good job opportunities. So, future any one kind of public transportation tool service provider ought consider how to satisfy working people working time need to shorten journey time to any working places or student learning time need to shorten jounrey times to any schools as well as let they feel comfortable to sit on comfortable chairs or provide free internet service to themselves mobiles , laptops, when they are sitting down or standing up in the kind of public transport . It is the important factor to influence any kind of public transport service in success.

Future Non-Manual driving vehicle How
Influences Public Transport Tool Passenger Need

Nowadays, artifical intelligent (non-manual) driving vehicles are invented, it may be accepted to any countries families to feel comfortable to drive on roads, because any people choose to buy any kinds cars, when any people choose to buy kinds of non-manual (artificial intelligent) vehicles, they do not need to use their hands to drive cars, because artificial intelligent (robotic auto control wheels, it means that robots can help human (drivers) to control wheel to drive to avoid any cars crash occurrence on the roads more easily.

If one day, non-manual driving robotic control whoole vehicles are invented in successful, whether it will persuade many different conuntries families choose to buy non-manual (robotic auto control wheel) vehicles, then it will cause bus, tram, train, underground train, road transport need will be influenced to reduce or even if non-manula boats are invented, whether it will cause ferry sea transport needs will b influenced to reduce. Hence, future non-manual driving vehicles or bats invention whether they will influence public transport tool of road and sea transport passengers number reduces. It is one interesting question. I shall attempt to discuss as below:

In fact, non-manual vehicles are very attraction, to excite any person chooses to buy to drive, because people do not need often touch wheels and touch foots button to control cars to move often forever, when robotic can be invented to help human to control car wheel and foot button, any person only needs to sit on his/her car, then the car can move rapidly, because any drivers is lazy, he/she hopes machine can help her/him to drive car on the road safely. So, he/she can read book or listen music or eatch mobile movie to enjoy his/her entertainment when he/she is sitting on his/her car.He/she will feel more comfortable and enjoyable when robotic can help him/her to drive car. So, robotic (non -manual driving vehicle) can encourage people to choose to buy cars because any drivers won't need to drive cars, robotic can help drivers them to drive on the road easily, when global any one family can own one robotic auto control (non-manual driving) car at least, it may influence these owning non-manula diriving vehicle owners do not feel need to pay any fares to buy road public transport tools of bus ticket, train ticket, underground train ticket , tram ticket to go to anywhere. So, it seems that robotic (non-manual driving) vehicles may influence future any road transport passengers number reduces , because traditional catching any kinds of road public transport tool passengers will be influenced to choose to sit themselves auto (non-manual) driving cars to go to offices to work, parents do not need to follow their sone/daughters to sit on themselves non-manual auto driving cars to go to schools, because their sons/daughters can sit on themselves non-manual driving cars to go to schools more easily. In holidays, they can sit on themselves non-manual driving cars to go to cinemas, music halls, breachs, theaters, shopping centers, gardens different entertainment places to enjoy their any leisure safely because robotic can help them to drive their cars on roads safely.

So, it means that robotic auto control driving cars can influence global every family to feel that they do not need to catch any kinds of public transport tools, e.g. bus, train, tram, taxi underground train to go to anywhere because robotic auto driving cars can help any one, he/she does not know how to drive car to go to anywhere safely. So, future any one won't need to learn driving car skill, when he/she likes to buy one auto driving car. So, in passenger public transport need view, non-manual driving cars will influence them to feel any kinds of road public transport tools can help them to go to anywhere conveniently, because themselves non-manual driving vehicles can help them to drive cars to go to anywhere conveniently. They only need to tell robotic that where they want to go, when they sit on their non-manual driving cars, then robotic knows whether where destination, they want to go, their cars will auto move on the road immediately. It is one exciting and enjoyable ourney when the driver does not need to drive his/her car on the road. So, it seems that robotic (non-manual driving) vehicles invention may bring negative influence to any kinds of public transport tools service needs to passengers , when passengers had owned one non-manual driving car at least.

Why and how non-manual driving car owners need

raise public transport quality on travel time and fare aspects

● How non human driving behavior can be influence by non-manual driving cars

In fact, impact of automated vehicless on travel mode preference, it can bring both trip purposes and distances aim raising need to any kinds of public transport service passegners. Because of technology penetration in the transportation system, the automated vehicle is set to be a future mode of transport, it may bring negative impact to future any kinds of public transport passengers needs, in special on the potential impact of these non-manual driving automated vehicles on travel behaior negative impact to public transport passenger behavior. Automated vehicles will influence future public transportation passengers feel it can bring more short time travel distances and short trip purposes more benefit than any kinds of public transport choices, e.g. bus, taxi, ferry, train, tram, underground tram etc. road and sea public transport tools, e.g. ferry, water taxi. It means that when future any passenger feels above these any one kind of public transport tool needs to spend longer travel time on journey distance and trip to compare future automated vehicles, then they will choose to sit on automated vehicles in preference, due to automated vehicles can help global any one person needs to go to anywhere rapidly.

So, automated vehicles may replace general traditional public transport tools in possible, when they are popular accepted in societies. On the other, instead of shortening journey travel distance time, (travel time) aspect, public transport fare, travel cost will be another influential factor to influence future public transport tool passengers to choose automated vehicles to replace to catch any kinds of public transport tools.

In fact, conventional cars and public transport s are perceivd as being the least attractive alternative in relation to in-vehicle travel time on short and long distance communting trips. So , future automated vehicle drivers (non -human driving) behaviors will be likely changed to prefer this mode for long distance leisure trips rather than short distance commuting trips by automated vehicles.

In fact, advanced technologies have revolutionized many aspects of human life, include the automated vehicle transport system. Also, transport system is one of the essential development aspect to particular , such as non-manual driving automation , vehicle aims to make trips safer, faster , more efficient, automated vehicles passengers and drivers can feel enjoyable to do themselves leisure behavior , e.g. read books, listen, music, listen mobile, watch laptop movies when any one does not need to consider whether their cars are safe to be driven , even any one needs to drive the automated car, because robotic can help them to control how to automatic drive this car on the road safely.

Robotic will bring confidence to let them feel that themselves cars are moving safely on the roads . In recent years, the concept of automated driving has been introduced as on outstanding platform for the next generation of driving systems that is expected to improve safety, traffic flows efficiency, reducing traffic jams occurrence chance, avoiding traffic accidents occurrence chance, e.g. avoid to crash any one person when he/she is walking across road or crach any car is moving on the road easily, capacity, accessibility , and reducing congestion through the application of some technologies , such as vehicle to vehicle and vehicle to infrastructure communication.

So, future automated vechicles can have good driving facility systems to be installed in their cars, in order to raise safety, rapid driving speed level to let any one to feel , when they are sitting in their automated cars, e.g. using cameras, sensors, global positioning system adaptive cruise control, light detection and ranging, and advanced driver assistance system, automated vehicles can steer the vehicle and drive it automatically when passengers delegate control to a computer. Absolutely, ny replacing the driver role with an automated driving system , future one automated vehicle is able to totally free up passengers under automation levels.

So, unless future any kinds of public transport tools may apply automated robotic automated driven system replace the bus driver, taxi driver, train driver, tram driver, underground train driver to raise automated driving system service improvement level to let any one passengers to feel. Otherwise, when automated vehicles are popular to be accepted to buy in any one country in global. Then, global public tansport tool passegners number may be influenced to reduce when global any one family owns at least one automated vehicle at themselves homes .

In other words, automated vehicles can bring thes benefits to let global any one household family feels, future automated vehicles users , they can mostly behave like passengers inside the vehicle, which implies that they will be able to multitask and productive by allocating the travel time to do other activities, e.g. reading, eating, working, drinking, watching movies, listening musics, even sleeping. So, automated vechicles will motivate humans to change non-humanly driven behaviors from conventional humanly driven behavior. This non-humanly driven behavior may be one main factor to influence or encourage future any one kind of public transport passenger won't choose to pay fare to buy ticket to catch any one kind of public transport tool again, because non-manual driven behavior may hel many lazy people do not need to consdierate how to learn to drive cars skills to prepare pass any road test in order to earn the driving licnece to permit to drive cars forever. When automated vehiclesa re popular to be accepted to replace manual-driven cars in societies.

Hence, automated vehicles could potentially change the traditional human driven vehicle market to cause their manual driven cars sale buyers number reduces, when the automated vehicle buyers number increases, also they can chance globa public transport passengers behaviors to reduce to pay fares to catch any kinds of public transport tools when automated vechicles users may sit on themselves automated vehicles to go to anywhere in short time rapidly and safely in any countries.

On conclusion, future global public transport service competition is serious, because instead of global passengers had began to compare whether which kinds of public transport fares are cheaper, more safe, shortening journey time between leaving place and destination, more comfortable feeling, e.g. clean and comfortable chairs , mre free internet service facilities in order to make any one kind of catching public transport tool choice in preference. On the other hand, future automated vehicles number will increase when traditional manual driven car users begin to believe that automated vehicles can bring more safe , more comfortable, more fee- time using, more leisure satisfactory feeling, more than traditional manual driving cars. Then, when global any one household family had made choice to buy at least one automated vehice to replace themselves car(s) at home. When, they are habit to sit in themselves automated vehicles to go to anywhere, however, short or long trip . Consequently, global any one household family won't feel any kinds of public transport tools may bring personal economic saving cost, comfortable, enjoyable, free-time using benefit to compare themselves automated vehicles . It will cause global public transport tools passengers number will reduce , when many different kinds of home automatic vehicles are purchased to replace manual driving cars by global household automated vehicle users. So, in passegner transport tool choice psychological view, automatic vehicles will be possible to replace future public transport service tools. So, any public transport service providers can not neglect how to desing and improve their facilities , charge reasonable transport fare, provide more comfortable, and enjoyable sitting feeling , even applying automatic driving system to replace human drivers in order to attract passegners ' catching need choice more easily.

AIRLINE AND AIRPORT TRANSPORT STRATEGY

In airline transport industry strategy, I shall attempt to indicate some useful strategies to help airlines to keep travellers number in order to avoid to reduce. I shall indiate as below:

● Airline Oil Price Variable Factor strategy

1.1 Positive social change influence to vehicle fuel consumers

What suitation is positive social change to vehicle fuel consumers. We are entering globalizational competitive society, such as airline fuel case, if the country, e.g. US is increasing vehicle consumers in this year, then US vehicle fuel demand will increase. So, the US vehicle fuel price will be caused to increase. Due to much vehicle fuel demand increases in US this year, so foreign fuel import and US fuel manufacturers will increase to supply to US for vehicle market in this year, due to many US vehicle consumers need to buy fuel to drive their vehicles in US. However, due to fuel natural resource will have limited number to be supplied to manufacture airline fuel, due to much fuel is used to manufacture vehicle fuel in US this year. So, it will cause airline fuel manufacturing and supply shortage challenge. Due to this year, US decreases airline fuel supply, but the US airlines demands fuel number is still increasing. Consequently, vehicle fuel increasing demand factor will cause airline fuel price to be rised in US this year.

For example, air tickets can be bought from internet, so travellers won't need to go to travel agent to buy conventienty. It is due to the global travel industry is increasingly competition. Thus, global travel industry competition will bring negative social change to influences fuel price rising because it will increase traveller numbers and airline flight times to fly. When, traveller's travelling desire demand numbers will be grown up fastly, then their online electronic-ticket buying or consumption behaviors will be rise. Thus, it will also cause online e-ticket price is decreased to attract many travellers to choose to buy e-ticket from online channel more than paper-ticket visiting travel agent channel. Thus, it is negative social change influences to cause fuel price rising due to plane flight flying times will increase and airline company will increase demand to buy many fuel to prepare to fly often. When fuel demand will rise, then the fuel sellers will rise fuel price in possible. Thus, airline industry global competition will being negative social change to influence fuel price raising up and air ticket price falling down to attract many traveller numbers to choose to buy among different travel agents.

Negative social change influence

What suitation is positive social change. I shall indicate economic growth example. When one country has better economic development in the year. Then, employers will have more effort to do businesses. Then, they will create many jobs to provide to the country citizen to do. When, these unemployed people have jobs to do, they will have extra income to save. They can spend extra to prepare to spend to enjoy their entertainment every year, such as travelling. Thus, the positive social change will influence traveller number increasing, then the plane fliging flying times will also increase, it will cause planes need to use much fuel to fly. The result, it will also increase fuel demand, but the fuel natural resource number will decrease , so fuel supply will also decrease. Finally, it will also cause fuel price to be risen.

Also, I shall indicate the financial risk of airline industry evidence from Cathay Pacific airways and China airlines against key determinants of which include interest rate, exchange rate and fuel price risk for the period of January 1996 year to December 2011 year. During this period, these key external factors which were the most serious influence to cause these two airlines choose to change their strategic behaviors.

Due to any these financial risks is difficult to predict and it was also changing often, these factors will also affect any airlines stock returns which arise from changing economic conditions, e.g. fuel price movements and fluctuations in exchange rates. These external unpredicted changing factors will attribute to the air tickets cyclical demand, capital investment, fixed costs of labor and landing rights to this global airline industry.

However, the relationship between fuel price and stock prices varies across economies. The effects of oil price changes in sub-sector indices, such as wood, paper and printing, insurance and electricity. In the past, on global stock exchange market was positively significant in 2011 year. Otherwise, with respect to the U.S.A. aviation industry, some economists suggested that global airlines stock returns were negatively to percentage change in fuel prices related to any airline firm value, e.g. Qantas and Air New Zealand were negatively share price growth to fuel price risk in the short term in the 2011 year.

Thus, it brings this question. Whether positive or negative social change will be one important factor to impact fuel price rising. I feel positive social or negative social change will be one important factor to impact fuel price rising. The reason is such as below:

Nowadays, airline transportation demands are increasing,

due to many travelers need to catch planes to travel as well as many cargoes need to be carried to planes to transport to different countries to sell. It seems aviation transportation industry is important to influence the health of the global economy growth nowadays. However, ignorance of internal or external market dynamics, catching travelers business can be detrimental to airline profitability more than carrying cargoes business. Because the demands of travelling different countries' travelers' consumption are still more than the demands of businessmen carrying cargoes in any countries every year. Thus, the travel industry will increase demand to human travelling business more than cargo transportation business. However, the cargo flying transporation demand will rise, due to many global fast speed post businesses are growing. Base on both global cargo flying transportation demand and travellers' flying travelling demand are increasing. Thus, the fuel demand will increase, but the fuel supply will be shortage. So, it will cause fuel price rising consequently.

How can positive or negative social change influence any airlines' air ticket prices to be risen or fallen? In fact, the increase in petroleum price can have chance to affect airlines in a negative manner because increased oil prices have resulted in the reduction of services operations, the number of airline schedules flights, even airline bankruptcies.

Thus, it seems that plan travellers and air flying cargo transportation both demand have been increasing. This social increasing demand change factor, it will be the most influential cause the bad effects to cause airline industry share price reducing or reducing air ticket price or decreasing traveler numbers more than the other factors influence, such as inflation, terrorism, oil shortage, bank interest rate etc. unpredictable external suitation factors.

To support this hypotheses, this are my research questions, such as : Does a combination of terrorism and price of petroleum significantly influence airline profit changing mostly? The alternative hypothesis was base on a significant relationship exists between terrorism, price of petroleum and airline profitability more than other factors, such as inflation, bank interest rate or air ticket price changing of these factors influence. I shall indicate that the first assumption was that terrorism has a negative effect on airline profitability and another assumption was that only external factors as oil prices or terrorism affect airline profitability.

Terrorisms attack influence

Whether terrorisms attack will influence fuel price rises up or falls down. I feel terrorisms attack to any country, which will cause plan fuel price falls down. Because travellers will feel dangerous and worry about their life safety when they catch the plan to enter the country if the country has serious terrorisms attack risk to cause plan crash accidently.

However the effects of oil price and terrorism on airline profitability was limited to a regional perspective, e.g. the terrorism attack of plane crash event to USA on 11 Sept. After the terrorism attack happened on USA 11 Sept. incident of terrorism attack was restricted to events of skyjacking, attacks on oil production, refinery and distribution. Thus, USA on 11 Sept. terrorism attack will cause oil price falls down , due to it will influence travellers fear death , so who will reduce times to travel to USA after 11 Sept. date terrorism attack occurrence at the year. The oil sellers will reduce oil sale price to attract many airline companies to buy more supply, due to airlines will decrease demand to buy fuel to provide planes to fly when the traveller numbers has decreasing and flying times will be decrease also. Thus, the fuel price will be decreased consequently after the terrorism attacks to any country.

Other types of terrorist activities, such as attacks on financial targets or senior government officials could have an adverse effect on the petroleum and airline industry. I think the disruption of the production or distribution of petroleum because of incidents of terrorism was costly in terms of loss of business and the inflationary effect on fuel dependent products or services.

In fact, some airlines have adopted more fuel saving technology, so whose fuel consumption would not use more than other non fuel saving technology airlines. So, the owned fuel saving technology airlines which will buy less fuel to use. It means that they won't need fear fuel rising to increase their expenditure because they only need to buy less fuel to use and their fuel demand won't fall , even fuel price has risen.

However, it seems fuel price increasing will not be the only factor to influence the airline industry's traveler numbers decreasing, due it is possible that the airlines need to rise air ticket price to riase their profit, sue to their fuel cost has risen. However, due to some airlines which have fuel saving technology, so which can avoid to use more fuel to provide planes to use and which fuel costs will be reduced, then which can provide cheaper air ticket fare prices to compare the non fuel saving technology airlines. The result will cause some non owned fuel save technological airlines will lose travelling customers in this global airline travelling market, also the non fuel saving technology airlines need to renew their fuel technology if which want to keep their competitive abilities to avoid to close down their businesses.

Can airline fuel self-organization avoid
fuel price rising cost

I feel one airline fuel self-organization can avoid fuel price rising to influence cost rising because it doesn't often buy any fuel from fuel suppliers. However, there are some airlines which are the characteristic of airline fuel self organization and they are present in that both of oil fuel production and providing flights service in airline industry. So, these airline fuel self organizations can control the oil fuel price by themselves. However, one airline fuel self organization is also evident in efforts by businesses acts of terrorism against economic targets by adopting proactive steps, such as airline and airport security. So, it seems airline fuel self organization can reduce the risk to avoid oil price raising and terrorism attacks to raise cost in airline industry risk management sector.

Beside, these airline fuel self organizations which have high technology of fuel efficient aircrafts, the use of one aircraft model, the adoption of direct routes versus customer loyalty programs and other operational cost reductions are strategies for increased profitability. It seems these airline fuel self organizations can solve oil price, terrorism etc. external factor influences to raise cost.

Instead of high technology of fuel efficient aircrafts and airline fuel self organization methods can solve terrorism attacks and oil price rising risks. However, I believe that there are other risks are caused to these airline fuel self organizations to raise their airline cost possibly. The risks include such as user factor, such as culture, tradition, education ; economic factor, such as costs, human resources and macro economic factor, such as political stability, economic development, educational policy, health policy, environmental policy. However, these risks occurrences are resulting in the relationship of cause and effect events. These events are not directly observable. Such as, the complexity of relationship between terrorism and airline profitability. Hence, if global airline industry can predict when those risks occur to do protective strategic behavior. It is possible that which can understand when these risk events will occur and to adopt their protective strategic behaviors to influence their outcomes to be positive to avoid any external risk threats on the long term. However, I think hierarchy, airlines fuel self organization efficiency methods which are as possible predictors of user preferences to avoid risk threat events to cause whose airline businesses cost rising to cause failure occurrences in airline industry.

Can tourism industry influence airline
profitability

In my study, I suppose terrorism and the price of petroleum both factors which had properties of distinct and interrelated close relationship to raise airline cost. Moreover, these variables (terrorism and the price of petroleum) displayed differentiation, self replication, efficiency and hierarchy which can cause risk events to airline industry. However, I also think the other internal and external threat factors of airline industry, such as inflation, bank interest rate, business model, service quality, airline fuel or plane engine technology, air ticket pricing, brand loyalty, airline strategic management, government policy and fuel hedging of these factors which can also raise the risks to threaten any airlines existence in airline industry.

There are two basic business models in tourism industry. They are network (full service) and low cost (discount) carriers. The network carrier model employs diversification strategy by increased domestic destinations, serving international routes, providing diverse seating arrangements (business, economy and first class), maintaining a complex system of offering high quality service. Otherwise, low cost (discount) airlines focus on lower air fares. To keep operating costs down, discount airlines offer shorter routes and provide point-to-point destinations rather than through sophisticated flights are primarily in domestic destinations. So, discount airlines operate a common model aircraft fleet, offer a single seating arrangement and cheaper flight services offered to compare network airlines. However, these two basic business models have their unique competitive abilities to provide any airlines existence in tourism industry nowadays.

In fact, natural resource of oil is decreasing in our earth. But as the same time, human demand is increasing and oil supply is decreasing, so it also causes the oil fuel price is increasing to supply to airline industry. It influences not only to airline industry, it also impacts of higher oil fuel price to tourism, such as expansion of airports are made based on expected demand increase.

Tourism has been proven to many adverse events, including terrorism, flight disruptions. Beside, the bad natural climate change influences, such as the volcanic ash cloud event occurred in April 2010 year. So, airline industry need to concern climate change because it will cause high fuel prices indirectly. For example, the event occurred the extreme increase in operating costs for airlines in 2008 year, due to unprecedented prices for aviation fuel also meant, that despite the introduction of fuel charges, so this event causes the global tourism industry recorded losses seriously. Even if alternative fuels become commercially available for airlines which are still likely to be more expensive than present aviation fuel.

Higher airfares in the future are likely to lead to reduction in travel and cause tourists to shift from more distant to closer destination. When some of the economic responses to higher oil prices are obvious assessing the overall economic impacts on tourism is difficult. However, long term changes in global oil price rises will be similar to global changes in other commodity prices, exchange rates and income. It is therefore important to consider the impact of high oil prices on tourism from a general equilibrium perspective rather than relying only on bottom partial equilibrium approaches.

However, I believe tourism and airline industries have close relationship, such as tourism and airline industries are likely to suffer in an environment of high oil prices. Given that tourism destinations receive tourists from a range of origins, it would be useful to understand of some countries are increasing oil prices than others. Such as the net oil importing countries are selling higher oil prices than oil exporting countries generally. For example, New Zealand is an oil import country to provide planes for international visitor arrivals, so its oil fuel price is usually higher to charge to NZ airlines because any NZ airlines need to pay to foreign countries to buy any oil more expensive price. So, NZ airlines usually charge higher airfares to its visitors to compare the other exporting oil countries' airlines. It will impact NZ has negative influence to domestic tourism industry as well as planes need will also be decreased , due to NZ charge high fuel price to cause air ticket price to be raised.

In economic theory, on income effects indicate negative

impacts on tourism demand, the exact effects of higher oil fuel prices for specific destinations are far from clear. However, airline industry's different market segments show different sensitivities to air ticket fares changes.

On the first hand, if the visitors are long destinations generally wealthier than average and therefore potentially less affected, as energy costs would be a smaller proportion of their income compared will be those from less wealthy groups. Thus, the more wealthier travelers who won't decrease travelling desire, even the fuel price raises to case the air ticket price to be increased.

On the second hand, oil prices don't translate into higher transport costs especially not on air routes that are highly competitive and that are maintained for strategic reasons. So, non air transportation industry won't influence customer number to be decreased easily.

On the third hand, many other factors shape tourists' decision making, including emotion drivers or those related to images, fashions and perceptions. Increasing environmental protection awareness of tourists could also be an important factor to influence tourism consumption, instead of oil fuel price raising causes air ticket fares raising factor to reduce traveler numbers. However, oil price raising reason causes also due to high use of cars, vans and domestic air transport in some countries, e.g. Hong Kong, China countries, there are many people like to buy cars to drive. So, the private driver numbers are increasing demand to cause these countries' oil fuel prices raise in the short time suddenly. It implies airlines need to consider their country car number whether is increasing or decreasing. If their country car number is increasing, it is possible to cause fuel price to be risen up because car demand is increasing to need to use more fuel and it has less supply of fuel in the year. Otherwise, if their country car number is decreasing, it is possible to cause fuel price to be fallen down because car demand is decreasing to need to use less fuel and it has more supply of fuel in the year.

Is fuel price rising only factor to cause airline risk in short term

In long run, fuel raising price will not cause risk to airline, due to implications of changes to supply and demand side conditions of oil fuel energy may differ qualitatively. For example, due to investment responses of producers, consumers and governments in alternative energy sources and more energy efficient plants, vehicles are supplied in order to achieve oil fuel price can't be risen seriously.

However, I believe oil fuel rising charge will be an important factor to influence global airline ticket fares to be increased in the short term to cause risk because oil fuel rising charge will be influenced to raise any airlines pressure from other unpredicted factor risk influences.

Firstly, on the bank interest changing factor, e.g. bank interest rate rising which only attract more bank saving. But it can not influence the bank savers who choose to reduce relax time to go to other countries travelling. Otherwise, when the bank savers can save more money to earn higher interest in banks, who will prefer to choose to use their saving to consume travelling. Due to who can earn higher interest rate after a period of saving time. So, I believe who behavioral travelling consumption will be raised when the banks will raise interest rate, then the bank savers won't choose to save more money in banks. So it is possible that who will withdraw more money to consume to go to travelling from banks. It seems bank interest rate changing won't influence bank savers' behavioral travelling consumption to be reduced.

Secondly, on the exchange rate changing factor, although any country's exchange changing will cause other countries' money value to be fallen down or risen up. However, it won't influence any travelers' behavioral consumption to be reduced seriously. Although, it is possible that the traveler won't spend too much to go to shopping when who travel to the another country and arrive the country. But, it is not possible to influence the traveler decides to reduce consumption to buy any air ticket to go to travelling in short time.

Thirdly, any country inflation also can not reduce travelers' travelling consumption easily because inflation can influence consumers who choose to buy cheaper foods and clothing and reduce entertainments in their every day life. But, one country's inflation can not influence it's citizen do not spend much travelling expenditure because travelers only spend one time or two times of travelling every year usually. So, the travelling expenditure rate of any households is not too much to compare daily essential expenditure.

So, it seems that bank interest rate and exchange rate changing and inflation won't influence any travelers' travelling consumption of decisions to be reduced easily in short time. Otherwise, if the oil fuel price raises too much, then global airlines' cost will be raised in long term. So, the airlines only choose to increase their air fare prices to aim to avoid loss possibly in long term. It seems that oil fuel raising price and bank interest rate and exchange rate changing and inflation factors will have direct influence airline income in long term.

● Methods to solve rising air fare prices to decrease

travellers'demand

Biofuels energy increases supply

I suggest these methods how to avoid the oil raising price factor to cause airline air fare prices to be risen to lead the risk of traveler numbers to be reduced as below:

The first method: Whether aviation fuel markets will have what benefits from biofuels supply to planes. I shall refer the scope includes trends in jet fuel price, airline response to fuel price, increases and volatility and environmental goals for aviation. The aviation fuel supply industry includes production, distribution and consumption of aviation fuel and it outlines players in the aviation fuel supply chain. For example, at each airport, fuel supply chain organization and fuel sourcing could differ with regard to the role of oil companies, airlines, airport owners and operators and airport service companies. However, major jet fuel purchasers are airlines, general aviation operators, corporate aviation and the military, with most of the jet fuel in global different countries demanders being used for domestic commercial and civilian flights carrying passengers, cargos or both.

Commercial aviation fuel efficiency has improved dramatically over time, largely due to aircraft and engine upgrades and operational and air traffic control improvements. So, it seems that fuel supply factor can influence airline fare prices majorly. However, jet fuel prices generally correlate with prices of crude oil and other refined petroleum products, such as diesel. So, increasing prices and the persistent price volatility of jet fuel markets import airline industry finances in any countries.

However, airlines use various strategies to manage aviation fuel price certainty, including financial hedges, increased vertical integration and adjustments in aircraft utilization and size to avoid the jet fuel raising price risk.

Investments in alternative aviation fuel could be a mechanism to diversity expose to the price of petroleum. It seems the use of alternative aviation fuel would serve to diversify the fuel mix to reduce the risk of jet fuel monopoly raising price threat. If a diversified fuel mix were to avoid either fuel raising price in short term or to avoid fuel raising price in long term. Potential benefits include reduced actual fuel costs from only choice of jet fuel supply increased price certainty and lessened fuel costs. This diversify could allow airlines to become more consistently profitable and to make other investments in their businesses.

So, biofuels have potential to meet aviation industry needs, possibly including managing risks of upward fuel price trends and fuel price volatility and avoid risks with greenhouse gas emissions. So, the aviation fuels market could use biofuels to reduce greenhouse gas emission and mitigate long-term upward price trends, fuel price volatility or both.

What are the challenges of high priced oil for aviation? In fact, nowadays not the resources of oil as such, but much more the insecurity of supply, due to geopolitical instability in combination with a tight oil market makes a scenario with much higher oil prices than the world is currently experiencing not unlikely.

Aviation is completely dependent upon oil as its fuel source. Since no practical energy substitute is readily available for commercial aviation, a scarcity of petroleum relative to demand will present a major aviation policy. In addition, efficiency gains, due to operational measures and new aircraft medium term. In particular, it has been demonstrated that the annual reduction rate in fuel consumption traffic unit is not a constant, but is itself also falling, in contrast to past estimates.

So, a high-priced oil scenario will have severe consequences for demand, airline revenues, the competitive position of airports and eventually airline networks, strategies and fleet development. In particular, transfer demand, short-haul and leisure traffic can be expected to be heavily affected by high oil prices, due to their relative high price sensitivity. Also, different countries' governments or/and airlines are valuable to research another new and potential biofuel energy to substitute oil energy to supply our planes to reduce the threat of oil monopoly supply to influence the cause of air fare raising prices. Because the elasticity is very high to travelers, when the travelers feel air fares are rising high or even low level to influence travelers who will choose not to buy the air tickets to go to travel easily.

Whether will the fuel (oil based inputs) risk be high to compare other costs, e.g. engineering maintenance, employees salaries, general cleaning, security office expenses etc. expenditures to airlines? If the probability-weighted upside effect on firm value when a risk is resolved favorably is greater the risk than the probability-weighted downside effect if the risk is resolved badly, then expected value work not be enhanced by hedging. So, the risk will be resolved badly to any commercial airlines.

Airlines are an interesting case because the direct effect of source of risk resides squarely within the no offset in revenue functions (unlike for oil producers, for example), so value effects from costs feed directly into equity value. Most directly, the risk source is fuel costs to commercial airlines. Jet fuel is of course, a mix product of crude oil, so airlines indirectly face oil price risk. There are reasons to expect that airlines' fuel costs might to convex in oil price (i.e. absent any hedging). For example, oil prices, being generally pro-cyclical in recent times, tend to be highest when airline demand is strong.

In conclusion, airlines are therefore apt to use more high priced fuel than low-priced fuel over time. Airlines can raise air fare benefit is limited by the elasticity of demand. Also, cost functions could be influenced from fuel cost corresponds to upturns in economic activity overall (due to demand pressures on oil related prices), so it causes that airline's capacity delivers their services given their level of fixed capital. The essence of airlines basis risk in the case of jet fuel is essentially the time profile of the refining margin between crude and jet fuel, or the time profile of the price differential between other refined distillates and jet fuel. Thus, it is far from clear that risk management with oil is sure to add value to any airlines. It seems the impact of airline energy and any countries' domestic or foreign airline passenger travel numbers which have direct close relationship.

Reducing terrorism occurrence

Can reduce terrorism occurence to reduce airline failure risk? It needs to judge to determine if a combination of terrorism and the price of petroleum significantly predicted airline profitability and which variable whether the further period was the most significant between the terrorism occurrence and the price of petroleum influence.

I suggest that different countries' governments or airlines need to collect samples of financial records from which country's any airline commercial passengers and cargo airlines on costs of fuel and any airline profitability. Also, gathering the terrorism data were comparison of terrorist attacks on petroleum in oil-producing nations, and incidents of high jacking aboard any country's aircraft.

When any countries' airlines or governments can judge whether the impact of airline energy and terrorism risk level is high or middle or low level. Then, which can use this sample data to measure how to do positive social change to decide either ought rise or reduce employment in commercial aviation industry, or ought need to invest other higher commercial activity in tourist and other travel related service businesses and when is the most right time to adopt of green technologies by the civil aviation manufacturing industry after the terrorism attacks occurrence to any country. It seems that any countries' governments or airlines which ought concern that the event of when the terrorism attacks will occur and gather past sample data to predict when the next time terrorism attacks event will be occurred and the risk will be high or middle or low level to influence global airline industry development.

Will airline industry's ticket price elasticity be influenced by demand and supply factor
In fact, the airline industry is largely dependent on the supply of the oil industry. Otherwise, the oil industry is inelastic. However, the increase or decrease of the price of airfare is directly related to the increase or decrease of the oil's price to fuel the aircrafts because there has no any new energy which can be substituted to oil fuel to airline industry.
So, it seems oil fuel producers are monopolies to control its sale price to be raised easily. Another factor that can affect airline industry to be directly targeted by a tragedy brought about by terrorism. The past four years, from 2001 year to 2005 year, there had been at least $40 billion worth of losses in the airline industry because of the September

11 date terrorism attacks in 2000 year. There had been an expected and significant decrease in the demand for the airline industry services because of the attacks that involved planes hijacking and crashing into key locations like the World Trade Center and the Pentagon in USA. Although, terrorism attacks can bring risk to influence fuel price rising in airline industry. However, this risk occurrence to airline industry is only that after the terrorism attacks occurred. It is possible that terrorism attacks won't occur again in the future.

Otherwise, our concerning ought be the greenhouse emissions and how it affects global warming. The air quality would be better once this new regulations are adopted. However, it would affect large airlines. So, it would increase the price of airfares because of economic fees that airline companies have to cover. Air pollution can give a negative impact on the domestic or oversea owned airline companies for long term. If airlines' planes can use clean fuel to fly, e.g. biofuel, then it will bring benefits to global airlines for long term.

On the positive side, the environment would be healthier as the earth's temperature would rise, and greenhouse effect would be dramatically reduced. This positive effect can come at a cost that is greater than most people perceive. On the psychology view point on travelers, who will be more preferable to catch planes to go to different countries to travel, due to the chance of air pollution and global environmental warm issues will be reduced to low risk to influence our health if planes can use biofuel to be energy to fly in the future one day.

It seems that spending expenditure to research other non polluted biofuel new energy is one solvable method to global airline industry in the future. To solve, any airlines or countries' governments or oil producers ought choose to spend more time to research new biofuel. Otherwise, the predicting when terrorism attacks event will be occurred, it is more difficult to predict the time more than researching to produce new biofuel energy method in the future. So, I recommend that researching the new biofuel energy or other kinds of energy to substitute the oil energy is the urgent behavioral economy which the airlines or oil producers or different countries' governments which need to concern nowadays.

● Boeing 747 manufacturing fuel cost strategy

For Boeing 747 air plane manufacture example, how it can help airline to avoid travellers number reduces. Boeing 747 air plane manufacture company how achieve air plane manufacturing strategy to reponse airline traveller number market changing. What is fuel conservation strategy to Boeing 747 air plane manufacturing firm? The cost index, (CI) feature of the flight manufacturing computer (FMC) can help airlines significantly reduce operating cost. However, many operators do not take full advantages of this powerful tool. What does CI ratio mean? The CI is the ratio of the time-related cost of an air plane opertation and the cost of fuel. The value of the CI reflects the relative effects of the fuel cost on overall trip cost as compares to time-related direct operating costs.

The equation form, CI= time cost-$/hour / fuel cosst -cents/ lb

The numerator of the Ci is often called time refrated direct operating cost (minue the cost of fuel). Items, such as flight crew wages can have an hourly cost associated with them, or they may be a fixed cost and have n variation with flying time engines, anxiliary power units, and air planes can be leased by the hour or owned, and maintenance costs can be accounted for an air planes by the hour, by the calendar or by cycles . As a result, each of these items may have a direct hourly cost or a fixed cost over a calendar period with limited or no correlation to flying time.

What does this air plane fuel, cost strategy advantages to airline companies? In the case of high direct time costs, the airline may direct to time costs, the airline may choose to use a larger CI to minimize time and thus cost . In this case, where most costs are fixed, the CI is potentially very low because the airline is primarily trying to minimize fuel cost. Pilots can easily understand minimizing fuel consumption, but it is more difficult to understand minimizing cost when something other than fuel dominates. So, the cost of the CI ratio. Although, this seems straight toward, issues such among the operating locations, fuel tankering, and fuel hedging can make this calculation complicated. So , this fuel consumption cost, air plan manufacturing strategy can help any airlines to reduce air fuel useful cost and waste fuel.

However, CI can be an extremely useful way to manage operating costs. Because CI is a function of both fuel and non-fuel costs. It is important to use it appropriately to gain the greatest benefit. Appropriate use varies with each airline, and perhaps for each flight.

How low fuel situations can bring less fuel consumed benefit in the more environmentally friendly flight? Fuel conservation strategy can help airlines significantly reduce operating costs. However, many operators do not take full advantage of this powerful tool. Cruise flight is the phase of flight that falls the largest percentages of trip time and trip fuel are consumed typically in this phase of flight, which also impact trip time and fuel significantly can often be avoided through appropriate cruise planning. This fuel conservation strategy includes these characteristics. These objectives which depend on the perspective of the pilot , dispatcher, performance engineer, or operations planner can be groups into five categories , such as:

1. Maximize the distance traveled for a given amount of fuel (i.e. maximum range).

2. Minimize the fuel used for given distance covered (i.e. minimum trip fuel).

3. Minimize total trip time (i.e. minimum time).

4. minimize total operating cost for the trip (i.e. minimum cost, or economy speed).

5. Maintain the flight schedule . The first two objectives are essentially the same because in both cases the airplane will be flown to achieve optimum feel mileage.

In addition to one of the overall strategic objectives for cruise flight, pilots are often forced to deal with shortage term constraints that may require them to temporarily abandon their cruise strategy one or more times during a flight. These situations may include:

Flying a fixed speed that is compatible with other traffic on a specified route segment. Flying aseed calculated to achieve a required time of arrival at a fix. Flying a speed calculated to achieve minimum fuel flow when holding (i.e. maximum endurance). And when directed to maintain a specified speed by a air traffic control. Hence, when the air plane faced with a low fuel situation at destination, many pilits will opt to fly LRC speed, thinking that it will give them , the most miles from their remaining fuel. Also, if fuel prices increase relative to other costs, a corresponding reduction in CI will maintain the most economics operation of the air plane. If however an airline experience rising hourly costs, an increase in CI will retain the most economical operation . For this reason, flight crews typically reserve a recommend CI value from their flight operations department, and it is generally not advisable to deviate from this value unless specific short term constraints demand it.

How it can help air planes to execute for maximum fuel savings efficiently? For example, but times have clearly changed. Jet fuel prices have increased over times from 1990 to 2008 year. At this time, fuel is about 40% oa a tycpical airline's total operating cost. As a results airlines are reviewing all phases of flight to determine how fuel burn savings can be gained in each phase and in totel.

Boeing 777-200 extended range and 747-400 and (long-range, e.g. short range e.g. 717, medium range, e.g. 737-800 with winglate commercail air planes can impact fuel usage. However, flap setting must be appropriate for the situation to ensure air plane safely. Higher flap setting configurations use more fuel than low flags configurations.

The difference is small, but at today's prices the savings can be substantial especially for air planes that fly a light number of cycles each day. Hence, top fuel conservsation strategies for flight crews include: Take only the fuel you need, minimize the use of the nuxiliary power unit, taxi use efficiencly as possible, take off and climb efficiently , fly the air plane with minimum drag, choose routing carefully, strive to mantain optimum attitude, fly the proper cruise speed, descend at the appropriate point, configure in a timely manner.

Fuel conservation is a significant concern of every airline . An airline can choose an approach procedure and flap setting policy that was the least amount of fuel, but it should also consider the trade off involves with using this type of procedure.

Hence, Boeing flight crew can earn benefit, when they fly or air planes, such as to conserve fuel and reduce noise and emissions or to accommodate speed requests by air traffic control. All of these are fuel consumption reducing strategy to airlines.

● How airlines and airports implement successful netwpork strategies

What is airline network strategy ? Network management includes route planning, scheduling optimization, airline business planning and data analysis . How implement airline network strategy, airlines need to evaluate strengths and weaknesses of the current network strategy, identification of additional potential, recommendations for adjustments, network integration, due to merger or cooperation. Fleet and capacity evaluation , analysis of estimated passenger volume over time combined with option aircraft size and frequencies for current and potential future rotes / markets; competition response, modeling of results as an impact of competitor's action and reaction; establishing best practice network managment for new carriers include: route selection, network planning, scheduling, airline business planning includes forecasting of revenues and costs. Finally, any airlines need to establish network planning, such as network optimization and development, traffic and revenue forecasting, market -and -competitor analysis, scenarios for profit-optimized networks include: hub-strategies, evaluation of aliances, cooperation includes: route joint ventures in industry environment.

● Performance measurement system strategy

Any airlines may apply performance measurement methods to design the indicates of performance. Different models and frameworks are excellence models. Any airlines hope to achieve useful performance meaurement strategy. They need to answer these kep questions: Who are the key stakeholders and what they want and need? What strategy airlines have to put into place to satisfy the key stakeholders' want and need? What critical process do airlines need if they want to implement this strategy? What capability do they need to operate and improve this process? What does cost leadership strategy mean? Competitive price is decided for customer . Indoneasia, Malaysia , India and China countries are implementing, it can provide cheaper workforces and the cost of production will be covered.

In aviation service industry, cost strategy , it much relevant to be applied cost carrier, such as Vigin Blus, Ryanair Airways are implementing . However, some airlines combined the low cost carrier and full service ,which is known as low fare limited services.

Innovative marketing strategy is not only how to carry many more passengers, but also how to enable significant reduction in the costs of distribution and marketing. Such a strategy is used as a competitive strategy of low cost tariffs . For example, low cost focus strategy serve tourists or groups with certain destinations, e.g. the flights are carried out by certain airlines.

There are also tourist groups who travel to certain tourist destinations. Passengers only are transported be the tourist destinations, thus departure schedule won't be a basic need, lower price of ticket and flexible departure schedule as well as comfortable cabin are still the standard.

Another improvement of performance method, it is market orientation, it is believed to give psychological and social benefits to the employees , in the forms of greater pride and sense of belonging, as well as greater commitment to the organization.

Another strategy improves to service performance, it is distribution management strategy . Everyone can be brought benefits. It may achieve these benefits: Raising passenger numbers, as some airlines and airports are running at near full capacity. The effects of disruption are only becoming compounded. Social media can help airlines and airports to tackle dissuption management and avoid damaging their reputation with consumers.

So, when discuption is solved. It can help airports reduce discuption cost and damaging their reputation with consumers . Innovation may include: airlines attempt to develop standard procedure for common disruption situations, responding to regulations, such as the delay rule and compensation for cancellations with faster, more proactive decisions, collaborating with air traffic control facilities, airports, themselves views of resources, identify available options.

● What factors influence cost-related management quality ?

Thus, the reduction of costs lies at the core of the low cost airline model, which aims to offer lower fares, elimating some comfort and services that were traditionally quaranteed, e.g. employed to refer to low-cost flight. The use of an airline booking system, the suppression of free-in-flight catering, the use of secondary airports connected through a point-to-point network, and the use of homogeneous fleets are only a part of the innovative choices made by low-cost airlines. However, these are main important factors to influence route structure, type and characteristics of the aircraft cost of labor and management quality . For example, if the airline's pilot, airline passenger service people, cleaners , all salaries can be reduced to employ. Then, the airport or airline's labor cost will be reduced and it can influence it's air ticket price to be also decreased.

When the airline's air tickets price reduces, it will bring competitive low air ticket sale price to win other airline competitors more easily. How air ticket sale attractive prices ? The airline's air plane type and characteristics,, whether they ae comfortable to let passengers catch in their whole trip time. Whether their air planes are new or old model ? Whether their air planes' facilities can satisfy passengers entertainment need, e.g. chair can be bed to let passengers to sleep, television or movie is attractive to watch, music is soft sound etc. psychological entertainment facilities can let the airline passengers feel satisfactory or not.

Final view is management quality, such as whether the airline or airport CEO's management ability performance is either excellent or good or general or poor . They can influence whole airline or airport front -line service staffs' service performance to let passengers or airport visitors feel their services can satisfy their needs when they choose to catch the airline air planes to fly to the country to travel or work, but the country's airport staffs' service performances and airport facilities will influence their revisiting to the country's airport or rebuying the airline's air tickets again.

The final strategy is flying route strategy. I believe that whether the flying route is attractive or not, it can influence passengers to choose the airline preference. Which factors determine choice of flights on the Dhaka-London route? How could the airline be able to cope with the competitive advantages of its major rivals in this flying route? How is the competitive environment for airlines operating in this route? How could the airline sustain its competitive advantage and what can it do to gain more market share in this route?

A successful and attractive flying route design needs to amend and adjust its flying route design strategies and capabilities as the airline firm goes through its flying route design life cycle, when changes in passenger's flying route choice preferences. Hence, any airline needs to know whether what its SWOT (strengths, weaknesses, opportunities, threats) before it decides to implement which flying route(s). Because manay flying routes choicew will be influenced by its current SWOT environment situation. For organization of new flying route to the UK airport from UK , e.g. London ciry airport, the HK airline needs to know whether what its strengths , e.g. customer loyalty, its strengths can provide the most rapid . The most cheapest, the more comfortable flying feeling from HK airport flys to UK London airport or from UK , London city airport flys to HK airport, its UK , London city flying route can provide competitive fare al promotion, extra baggage allowance, airline brand image , whether is famous to UK travellers, providing online seats reservation for any UK , London flights services, airline organization size and airline brand , whether it can get travelling passegners, loyalty or confidence either to fly to UK , London city from UK city airport, or flying to HK city from UK, London city airport, providing regular UK , London flying route schedule, network presence how much UK flying route cost cutting, Uk air planes' aircrafts facilities whether are enough to satisfy HK or UK to catching the airline's air planes flying entertainment needs. Does it one new route development opportunity of direct flughts from HK airport to UK , London city airport. HK air port has enough terminals number to let facilities to provide passengers stay in HK airport when UK , London city travellers arrive HK airport? Does HK airport lacks technologica facilities to satisfy new UK , London city airport flying route development , e.g. providing enough spaces to let air fleets stay in HK airport, aircraft manintenance whether is enough? Does HK airport encounter shortages of experienced front line counter service staffs to serve UK , London city travellers in airport? When the seasonal time is holiday travelling time for UK visitors, is UK new flying route rising fuel cost? Does new entrants to develop another UK , London city flying route from HK? Has new UK , London city from HK flying route , these weaknesses , such as lacking enough resource to develop another another new flying route or no direct flight or long hour flight after the HK airline developed the new UK , London city flying route to the HK airline from HK airport. Has new Uk, London city flying route development enountered these threats: strong competiton, high interest and UK foreign currency exchange rates, raising fuel cost, economic recession decline in the UK airline industry, environmental pollution etc. issues influence UK travellers choose to travel to HK desires. So, SWOT analysis must be needed to consider in order to develop any new flying route in order to avoid servious high cost expenditure loss to any airlines.

So, above these tangible , e.g. fuel cost control , route choice, network cooperation choice and intangible, e.g. service performance factors can influence whether the airline's network cooperation strategy, route choice strategy or low cost strategy can succeed or fail. So, airlines or airports can not neglect these factors to be revised in order to achieve any strategies in success more easily.

Economic Environment Influences Airport
service performance

Airline employee positive emotion method
    Emotional labor factor
    Airline service industry, front line travelling passengers service workers' emotional challenge concerns cabin crew and airline ground service employee whose service quality or performance how to serve travelling passengers in order to reach service level or satisfy their service performance needs to be accepted. So, how to influence airline service labour individual emotional matter which will be one major factor to let travelling passengers how they feel satisfactory to the airline service.

    The question concerns how to let airline service cabin crews and air ground service employees build long term good emotion to serve their airline travelling passengers. Because
bad emotional airline service labors will damage the whole airline employers' loyalty as well as reducing travelling passengers number in possible.

    Will a lot stresses at work cause bad emotion to airline ground service employees? The hospitality industry comprises of travel and tourism and the major segments include lodgings and cuisines (hotels, restaurants), transport(airlines, rentals, cruise and railway companies), travel and tour operators. All of these related travelling industries' employees , they are emotional labor, whose service performance or service attitude will influence future potential travelling passengers' airline choices to the airline operating servicer again. Any airline service employees in these service sector industries, have to interact with their travelling clients, be its customers on a regular emotion reflecting basis. So, they must be patient to listen any travelling passengers' enquires in order to help them to solve any problems considerably.

Emotional labor is managing one's feelings to generate a publicly accepted facial and bodily display of emotion. Emotional labor is an expression of emotion for a wage. Jobs involve face to face or voice to voice interactions with clients (travelling passengers), jobs demanding the employee to produce and alter an emotional state in other person, and jobs allowing the employer to implement certain amount of control over the emotional activities of the employees, produce or create emotional labor among the employees.

Thus, long time bad emotional airline front labors number increasing, it will influence the airline whole service member performance to be its airline passengers. However, many airline organizations have their owning set of norms or policies that determine these feeling rules. These are specially seen in customer service industries. IN long term, these strict policies will let airline front service staffs feel stress or pressure, because they won't feel to be punished in possible, e.g. without salary continue increasing, dismissal (lose jobs), changing to another position to do more simple or boring job duties, if they are discovered that their working service performances are not satisfied to their airline employers in any time.

So, strict airline organizational policies will be one strict or pressure emotional regulation to any airline front service staffs. This emotional regulation refers to a person's capability to accept and understand his or her experience of emotions to get involved in healthy strategies in managing emotions which are uncomfortable whenever required, when they need to contact their airline passengers every day. In fact, it has possible that they will accept unreasonable complaint from their airline passengers, even they perform very good or they have help their airline passengers to solve any enquiries when they feel any needs, they stay in airports any time. So, it has close relationship among airline front service staffs' emotions and the airline's policy as well as their service attitude. Thus, good airline policy will build good airline service staffs' emotions and good service attitude or service behaviour to serve their airline passengers every day in possible.

Any airline organizations can not neglect to consider how to build (keep) good airline front labor emotion issue. Because they are any airlines' representatives, if they can build good

images to let the airline the airline passengers to feel. Then, it will influence many airline passengers to choose to buy the airline tickets to replace other airlines because they like its front airline front staffs' services. SO, any airline organizations need to consider front service staffs' health status and definite psychological or mental diseases more than physical diseases, because many airline front service staffs only need to serve their airline passengers and they do not need to move any heavy things in airports in general. They need to spend more time to contract their passengers more than any things. When their passengers give their passports or/and any related travelling documents, e.g. air tickets to them to check in to find whether they can allow to enter airport restrict areas, and if they give their luggage to them, they also need to help them to measure its size and weight heavy to decide whether they need to pay extra fee and their luggage are permitted either to keep to them together to enter the air planes to fly or separate air planes to fly to destination. So, they need to make accurate judgement need to avoid any error occurrence. They do not allow to do any wrong judgement or error in order to be complain by their airline passengers often. Hence, any airline organizations need have good method to help their airline front service staffs to avoid to do any wrong judgements in order to influence any flights delay or customers' complaints , due to their personal wrong judgement to their passengers cause in possible.

Thus, any airline organizations require to enquire themselves these questions: Is there any influence of emotional labor (surface acting and deep acting) on the general mental health or psychological disease of airline employees? Is these any difference in the experience of emotional labor across demographics (age/gender/mental status/work experience of airline employees influence their service performance? Because above any one factors , such as every airline front service staff individual age, airline service experience, marital status of these factors will influence their emotions to be good or bad to serve their airline passengers every day. Hence , any airline organizations need to investigate every airline front service employee individual background in order to arrange the most suitable policy to train their front line or ground airline service staffs' skill in order to let them to feel less stress or pressure
or they can feel happy to enjoy to serve their airline passengers.

On conclusion, reducing airline front or ground service staffs' psychological stress or mental pressure issue which will be the most effective or the best solution to assist them to raise confidence to serve their airline passengers in airports in long time. I believe that it is the most rapid psychological solution method to assist any one airline front or ground service staff to raise service level in short time.

Airports service environment factor

The environment of airports service environment for the airline services, which will also influence travelling passengers' travelling destinations and travelling frequent times choices. The airport price factor includes income growth, aviation technology and local economic / geographical features of the country's domestic or overseas airports both. IN fact, airports, airports are indeed two sides businesses, it has commercial relationship between both airlines and passengers. So, airports' pricing will influence passengers' travelling demands to the airlines in the country. Any countries' airport(s) need(s) to respond how to help themselves country airlines how to increase passengers number and airlines choices in order to achieve attracting traffic on frequent air planes flying aim. Because the country's travelling passengers number increases , it will influence the country's airport(s) ' income increases indirectly, instead of the countries' any airlines themselves incomes.

Hence, any country's airport(s) will be one good platform to let travelling passengers to stay in the country's airport(s). It means that id the country's airport(s) can build good service image and reasonable products sale price and comfortable shopping environment to attract any countries' passengers feel comfortable and worth to stay in themselves countries' airport(s), when they need to transfer air planes to stay in the country's airport, e.g. one hour to five hours short time, even overnight long time staying. However, if they
feel the country's airport(s) are(is) more comfortable and

clean to stay, less noise, as well as they have enough chairs to let them to sit or sleep and large area to let them to work in the airport ground floor.

Moreover, the country's airport(s) can have enough restaurants , bookshops, any electronic or other kinds product shop[s, even cinema etc. shopping or entertainment services to satisfy
the passengers whose eating needs, entertainment needs, shopping needs in the airport. Then, I believe that the country's airport(s) can help itself airlines to attract many passengers
to choose to increase travelling times to the country frequently. For example, when the country's airport passengers feel that the airport restaurant food concessionaires will probably provide enjoy positive external gains from having more flights at the airports, additional or better eating facilities are unlikely to provide external benefits to the airlines by stimulating many more passengers with local origins or destinations to use the airport. I believe these airport restaurants can influence the choices of transit passengers whether which country will be their transfer air plane's short journey staying airport destination to fly to their final destinations. Although, transit passengers usually stay to the transfer air plane airport in short time, but they hope that these any one transit staying airport can have any restaurants to provide good taste food to them to eat when they feel hungry, if the transfer air plane country's airport can provide enough restaurants and they can have different food taste choice and reasonable price. Then, the airport's restaurants may attract many short time transit passengers to choose to eat their food, even many passengers will like to choose the country's airline to buy tickets to stay short time to wait to

transfer another air plane to fly to their final destination to replace another country's airport to stay short time.

Hence, it seems that any countries' airports' entertainment, eating and shopping service environment will influence any countries transit passengers whether they ought either choose to stay short time this country's airport in prefer or another country's airport to stay short time in prefer in order to decide to buy the country's airline air ticket for transfer airplane to another destination. Hence, any airports service environment will influence any countries passengers how to make transit airport destination short time staying choice.

However, I also suggest that an airport will place a lower revenue -over cost burden on that side of the travelling market that benefits the other the most. Assuming one passenger
can earn benefit enjoyed by airlines from an extra-passenger using the airport, the airlines will be willing to pay up to this amount to increase passenger enjoyed benefit feeling.

The airport can extract rent from the airlines up to above their allocated costs for providing the airport short time staying platform (transfer air plane short time staying airport) for eating, entertainment, shopping need service of increasing their destination arriving passengers or transfer another air plane passengers number base. This involves transferring the external benefits derived by airlines from additional passengers using the transfer airport to the another destination airport.

On the another view, from a airport location choice perspective, locating or expanding an airport near a city center can reduce or at least contain passenger access costs . But, because land is like to be more expensive, the airside costs to airlines are serious higher and if the various other external costs of aviation are included. Hence, countryside or the airport is built far away from city center in the country. This location is one reasonable location choice, because it can reduce noise to influence people who are living when air planes are often flying or landing on the airport and the rent cost to the airport's any business renters will be influenced to reduce. Then, their food , product or entertainment service prices charge to the airport consumers will also be reduced. Thus, any airports ought nor neglect their building location choices in any countries because they will influence airport business renters sale prices.

Lean maintenance repair and manual
error factor

Any airlines must need air plans to catch passengers to fly to travel. So, any air plans will need often to fly. Every flight will need long time to fly, e.g. short trip needs to fly less than five hours, even long trip needs to fly more than five hours, even ten hours. If many passengers choose the country to travel, the air plan needs to fly
frequently to catch every flight passengers to go to the travelling destination frequently. So, any airlines air plans often need to check whether they have any engine machines has broken, need to be repaired in possible in order to let passengers feel the airline air plans are safe. If the airline's any air plans have occurred any accidents when they are flying, even the accidents cause any one passengers hurt, even death. Then, these flying accidents will let passengers feel life risk to choose this airline's any air plans to catch to fly. IN special, long time trip(s) flight(s). So, lean maintenance and engine check is needed to

consider for any one airplane to any airline in order to improve efficiencies and minimize costs, maintenance, repair,
and overhaul services in the aviation industry sector, even avoiding any flying accident occurrence or reducing serious flying accidents occurrence chance to bring any one passenger
hurt, even death when they are catching any one of the airline air plans to travel. Thus, any one of airline safety is one important successful factor to any airlines.

Instead of passenger safety aspect, the flying logistics safety factor is also important. The central tenet of the lean to a flying process can mainfest in a variety of ways , as over stalled
and underused inventory and misallocated labour, time transportation and logistics. From a customer's perspective, value-added activities are necessary and customers are willing to pay for activities(Bamber, 2000, Glass, 2016). For example, improvements caused by lean introduction in aviation industry in order to avoid misallocated labour time, increasing number of old broken tools, and obsolute jigs and fixtures. Aviation MRO services have been reported by the MIT Lean Aerospace Initiative (2005) to result in:

(1) Set up time: 17 to 85 percent improvement.
(2) Lead time: 16 to 50 percent improvement.
(3) Labour hours: 10 to 71 percent improvement.
(4) Cost: 11 to 50 percent improvement.
(5) Productivity: 27 to 100 percent improvement.
(6) Cycle time: 20 to 97 percent improvement.
(7) Airline airplane manufacturing factory floor space: 25 to 81 percent improvement.
(8) Travel distance (people and products): 42 to 95 percent improvement.

(9) Airplanes engine inventory or work in progress: 31 to 98 percent improvement.

(10) Scape, rework , deflects or inspection: 20 to 80 percent improvement.

Hence, any airlines' airplanes need to be achieve any one of above improvement at least percent level in order to keep airplane's accident occurrence chance to the least level.

Moreover, airplanes' pilot employees their flying experiences or flight numbers factor is also important to influence airplane safe flying issue. Because if the pilot has less flying

expereince or he is not proficient pilot, or his flight number is less. This pilot's individual flying factor will also influence the airplan's safety when he is driving the airplane.

So, any airlines need to consider how to train any one of pilot to be one proficient pilot, because id less experienced pilot , he/she is not proficient to drive any one airplane to fly. Then, the flying accident occurrence chance will also raise. It is one critical successful factor to influence passengers' confidence to choose the airline's airplanes to catch, instead of maintenance repair and checking engines factor.

On conclusion, raising travelling passengers' safe confidences factor will be one critical successful factor to influence any airlines' services level, because flying safety issue

must be one important matter to be considered to any passengers when they decide to choose the airline's airplane to catch to fly to any destinations. If one airline can not guarantee any flying accidents won't occur, to cause any passengers hurt or death. Then, any passengers won't have confidence to feel its others services level can satisfy their basic flying enjoyment

needs. Due to passengers' life cost must be no worth calculation more than other service cost. When they choose to catch the airlines' any one airplane to fly to the another destination form the

country's airport. Hence, the influence of human factor in airport maintenance factor will influence any airlines' services feeling level to their passengers because human factor is one of the safety barrier which is used in order to prevent accidents or incidents of aircraft.

Therefore, the question is to which extent the error caused by human factor is included into the share of errors that are made during aircraft maintenance, such as flying accidents, incidents, injuries, death, damages related to aircraft operation and maintenance. More airlines' detailed analyses have led to the knowledge that it is necessary to study the

interrelation of repair people, machines, airline factory maintenance and manufacturing working environment, and the air planes production processes. Human is the key factor production

process and in the process of operation of technical means since gives new value to the object of any one airplane manufacturing process.

As a factor, the human is not perfect and introduces unintentional error in the system. It is important to develop a system of ever identification and to work constantly on error

prevention. The works and activities on aircraft maintenance can produce hidden and active errors on the aircraft. Hidden errors are a type of errors that are seemingly invisible during aircraft

flying. Active errors are errors that occur immediately and

result in immediate aircraft damage or injury , even death to any travelling passengers.

Hence, non human or without human factors will be less number to compare human factors to cause any flying incidents or accidents occurrence easily, e.g. damaging engine, old engine (no renew engine), fire, crash etc. different kinds of causes. However, the main causes of human errors to cause any flying accidents may include: lack of communication between the pilot(s)

and airport airplane landing staffs, complacency (assessment of work according to previous working experience), lacking of flying knowledge to the pilot, distraction, lack of

team work, fatigue, lack of materials and technological support), pressure on the work performer, lack of assertiveness (lack of self-confidence or technical approach to work),stress (working under pressure), lack of awareness etc. different human factors. Any one of above human factors will influence any flying accidents cause.

Moreover, instead of human factor, the flying working environment which refers to the space and place for work as well as the conditions of work factor will also influence human

error occurrence increasing chance, e.g. time pressure, equipment and tools enough number supplies, night shift, all of any one work environment factor will also influence human error

occurrence increasing chance in any flight flying. However, the factors that lead to cause of maintenance error may be caused from wrong information system supplies of equipment , aircraft

manufacturer, wrong working equipment and tools, wrong design of aircraft equipment and parts, incorrect working task arrangement, lacking technical education to the aircraft maintenance

workers, employee's bad personality, poor aircraft factory manufacturing working environment, poor airline company organization structure, working management and control and poor

communication etc. different manual or non manual factors.

Hence, all of above any one non manual factors will also raise manual error factor to cause any flying accidents occurrence chances. However, if any airlines hope to satisfy their passengers' flying service level. They must consider non manual and manual both factors for aircraft lean maintenance repair service aspect.

Influence of airside and off airport to airport geographical choice factor

What does airport airside means ? It includes a system of three components: runways, taxiways and agron-gate areas, on which aircraft and aircraft support vehicles operate. It brings this questions: Why can airport airside operation influence passengers feeling to the country's airport and airline services? How does it influence airport ground service staffs' service performance?

In fact, this airside airport physical area choice has direct relationship between aircraft and apron gate areas of the terminal processing of passenger and cargo. They are major factors to influence operations on runway component. It means that airport ground service staffs' service efficiency, used for the passengers and air fright catching any airplanes processing.

Hence, in a geographical sense, landside and airside capacity on how designing and building og geographical area can bring indirect influence to passengers. They need to enter or indirect influence the airport , in special, many flights are staying on the airport runway as well as many passengers need to leave from the airplanes or enter to the airplanes in the same time on the airport boundary. Hence, if the airport has good airside design , then many passengers will feel convenient to leave or enter the airport from the airside areas.

Airports are perhaps truly intermodel terminals in the transportatoin system. They provide an intersafe among air highway, rail and even water way travel. They are an important part of the medium and long distance intercity transportation system in our future transportation tools. Hence, it has enough reasons to support airside geographical airside and off airport factors can influence an airport and its airline flying service providers on its capacity as well as how it's capacity can influence passengers' satisfactory level when they arrive the country's airport. Hence, airport's congestion growth problem that is needed to consider to any airports because when one airport 's congestion is growing.

It will influence passengers service satisfactory level to be fallen down in possible, e.g. capacity is increased by the addition of a new access road, such as additions provide a major increase.Thus, the stair step growth, it will cause congestion growth because if the airport had used many areas for stair step growth and passengers will have less space to let them to walk on the ground and their airport congestion feeling will also increase when passengers are staying to leave the airport or waiting for check in or check out or waiting to transfer another airplane in the country's airport.The major airside factors to influence travelling passengers whose airport service feeling may include as below:

Availability of enough land for expansion for runways, availability of aids to navigation and air traffic control techniques that could result in reduction of separation between aircraft , noise, aircraft mix, load factor, exclusive use and use of gates , enough airside and outside facilities, availability of airspace, whether aircraft large size is enough capacity and where is location of gates, staffing, equipment freight, environmental protection regulation, and community attitudes toward airside operation.

Thus, whether the airport has enough facilities to satisfy passengers staying in its airport service need, it will have indirect influence further passengers increasing or decreasing number problem. For example, if the airport terminal functions are spread over a large geographic area, access and facilities have to be expanded to accommodate the spread-out configuration of the terminal or if terminal facilities are grouped together, the access facilities can be congregated into a smaller geographical area.

The capacity of the landside is a function of the terminal design , which has a major influence on the relative to between airside and landside capacity. Also, these off airport factors can also influence landside capacity, they may include: off airport parking, off airport terminals, urban development pattern, multiple jurisdiction, financial resources etc. issues. The sub factors of the off-airport access functions , they can influence passengers' services feeling to the airport. They may include: user and vehicle characteristics, e.g. occupants per vehicle, separate and preferential guide way subsystems, roadway traffic management, access link to major transportation , transportation connections. All of these airside and off-airport facilities will influence passengers' servicing feeling when they arrive any countries' airports. Hence, any countries' airports ought not neglect any one of these minor airside facilities of inside airports to outside airports both.

The another geographical choice airport building issue, it is also one critical factor for how the development of airport cities. It will influence passengers' service feeling to any country airport. The questions may include: Why may any country need to develop an airport city? Can it bring economic benefit and attract many passengers to choose to travel the country? Can the airport city reform to raise airport service performance or service level? Airports have become new dynamic centers of economic activity, incorporating several commercial and

entertainment services inside passenger terminals, when developing a hotels and accommodations , office complexes, conference and exhibition centers or leisure facilities choices for leisure passengers and business passengers both.

Airport-centered development may occur at different spatial scales (from the micro scale of the passenger terminal to the regional or metropolitan scale), thus assuming different

shapes and mainfestations. Different concepts to address these developments can be found in the " airport city", airport corridor, and aerotopolis (Guller, M. & Guller, M, 2003).

I shall explain how airport city concept can help to raise passenger service performance feeling in airports and airlines as below:

In general, airport passengers hope airports ought provide these different kinds service and achievement the lowest satisfactory service quality or performance level to

let
them to feel, such as air transport needs have complex airport -neighborhood interactions (in what concerns an eventual development towards the concept of airport city) requires the
identification of thes takeholders involved and an awareness of the relationships between them. Any airport's main task needs to provide traveling, air transport, shipping, entertainment services to the dual market of airlines and travelers. As such, its primary interaction consists of the supply and demand relationship with the users stakeholder group (passengers and airlines), which results in broad terms in the airports aeronautical revenues. Furthermore, non-aeronautical (commercial) revenues also result from the interactions between airport and users, namely from agents such as cargo and passengers oriented organizations who pay rents or concession feeling to the airport authority, depending on the commercial arrangements binding these agents.

Thus, one successful airport city, it ought provide good neighborhood transport service to travelling passengers, e.g. bus, taxi, ferry etc. public transportation service. It aims to avail any airport passengers can catch any one of these public transportation tools to arrive airport or leave the airport easily. It also needs to provide hotel, conference service for business visitors as well as retail shops, cinemas for shopping visitors or entertainment visitors when they are staying in the country's airport(s). Also, it ought provide facilities to any cargo -oriented organizations to deliver any cargo in short time rapidly. So, one airport's any neighborhood facilities have relationship to influence any passengers and airport organizations' service performance feeling between different user agents including: service provision (e.g. between passengers and businesses), business transactions, supply and demand (e.g. between public transport providers and passengers and passengers or visitors) and employer-employee relationships (businesses and workforce , such as airport airline ground service workers). Because if they feel that they can work in one comfortable airport working environment, they will feel happy and enjoyable to serve their passengers more everyday. It means that any airports' facilities will have indirect relationship to influence airport ground service workers' psychology to feel either enjoyable or hate to work in the airport environment often.

On conclusion, airports ought need to consider themselves airside and off airport facilities whether they have enough supplies and innovate their facilities to be better , even perfect in order to satisfy any airport visitors, travelers, user organizations and airport ground service employees to enjoy to work and use their services if they hope their service level or performance is satisfied to their service needs for long term.

Influencing air connectivity to service quality factor

Can air connectivity growth decreases travel costs for attracting travelling passengers, consumers and businesses and facilities global productive growth? This seems to be particularly an issue when airport capacity is scare or when new airports are added to an existing airport system. What is air connectivity ?

Why does air connectivity raise passengers services? How to measure air connective service?

When direct and indirect connectivity relate to the airport connectivity available to local travelling passengers, any airports ought need to raise extra airline services to raise service quality , e.g. cheaper air ticket price, in-flight service extra service provision, e.g. comfortable and clean and quiet air port waiting environment

service provision and feeling. However, passengers will generally prefer direct, non-stop connections over indirect air connectivity service.

Air connectivity service can assist airlines to raise competitive effort an offer and they provide access to the many destinations with too little demand for a direct flight, such as minimum connecting time differs in quality , due to in-flight time differences, the inconvenience and risk of missing a connection and transfer time for direct or indirect flights. Hence, any airlines can reduce passengers indirect or direct flight in-flight time to wait airplanes arrive to catch when they arrive any airports. This air in flight waiting time shorten service will attract many passengers to choose the airline to catch airplanes if its inflight waiting time to airport passengers is lesser than other airlines' in-flight waiting time in any airports. It can raise airline service quality, due to the airline has many passengers feel in-flight waiting time is shorten than other airlines often.

In fact, airport connectivity is one good concept method to raise passengers' satisfactory service level. One of the important factors for the connectivity of airports may include: The size and economic strength of the local catchment area how drives outbound demand, size and economic activities as well as tourism attractiveness are an important cariable factor in explaining inbound demand (including the propensity to flying demand), landside accessibility drives the size of the catchment area that airlines can serve from a particular airport within a certain landside travel time, apart from the socio-economic variables factor, also cultural , political and the historical ties play a role in explaining demand the origin-destination level factor. All of the research on the factors that explain air level, demand at the origin-destination or airport level is widespread, including gravity modelling (e.g. a bed at al., 2001) and regressions on aggregate

airport demand (Dobruszkes, 2011). All of any one factors may be airport connectivity service to influence passengers' service feeling level in airports and airlines both service quality.

ON airport visit costs aspect, airlines also need to consider airport visit costs in their route development strategy. Visit costs may also influence passenger choice behavior when

airlines pass on higher/lower charges to the passenger through air fares. Although, airport visit costs generally represent a limited share of an airline's total operational costs, this share can be more significant for short haul flights as well as fair airlines. All of any one these airport charges and passenger fees variable may influence passengers airlines choice. They may include:

Fees variable, landing charge, parking charge for their vehicles or aircraft, passenger luggage charge, security charge, boarding bridge charge, noise charge, emission charge, airport development service increasing charge, check -in charge, terminal charge, cargo charge. So, if any one of these charges influence the airline ticket price rises, it will influence passengers' air ticket purchase choice to the airline in possible.

On airport service levels aspect, for keeping and attracting passengers, airlines and airports need to compete with services that improve the passengers experience. Such

service
factors concern for immigration and luggage, but also
relate to the terminals, waiting transfer another air plane
time, shopping facilities, toilets, atmosphere and space
cleaniness, friendliness of staff and availability of delicated
lounges. Together they determine the image of an airport
and its perceived value by passengers and airlines.

On airline routes development aspect, it can also
influence passengers choices to the airline, e.g. Australia
airline had developed long route to England destination.
Any Australia
passengers can fly to England route directly. They do not
need to transfer another air plane to go to England.
Although, flying time is above 12 hours long time, but it can
bring available to
passengers. They do not need to spend time to wait another
air plane to transfer to go England in Australia any airports.
THus, airline route development strategy airline planners
require detailed, accurate information to make new route
decisions, but airlines usually do not have the resources
to fully evaluate every new route market. So, they need a
sound well articulated business case, can convince airlines
to introduce new air services, as well as airport /
destinations can influence the airline planning process.

For example, Interviewer indicates that new routes are a
huge investment and risk to an airline in airline economic
view point, if the airline had not gathered any data to
evaluate
whether the new route is worth to develop and predict
passengers' new route choice behavior. It assumed 75% lead
factor will influence any new route development in success.
It indicates these different aircraft type and seats per flight,
annual passenger requirements data for these aircrafts:

Boeing 747 aircraft needs to satisfy 400 at least seats per flight and annual passenger requirement need 219, 000, aircraft airbus A340 aircraft needs 280 at least seats per flight and annual passenger requirements need 153,300 , Boesing 767 to 300 aircraft needs 220 at least seats per flight and annual passenger requirements need 120, 450 . Boeing 737 to 700 aircraft needs 76,650 and regional Jet aircraft needs 100 at least seats per flight and annual passenger requirements need 54,750.

Hence, any airlines need have route priorities strategy before they decide which new flight route(s) will be developed , in order to achieve airlines add service in order of expected profitability, different airlines have pursued different strategies, destinations can move up the priority board with: solid research and analysis (always) and incentives (sometimes).However, any airline questions for new routes may include as below:

What is the current, actual market for a potential route? How much can my airline stimulate the flight flying market?

How will the competition react?

How much market share will achieve?

How will be the connectivity contribution?

Will the new route be a financial success?

Hence, any airlines need to reduce uncertainty and risk, before they decide to develop any new route market.

The air service development process may include as below:

Step one: market assessment, required a quantify the time size of the existing air travel market

step two: strategy, deficiency analysis and detailed route analysis step three: business case analysis, packaging and presenting the information to airlines

step fourth: evaluate and negotiate airline incentives

It is the final steps an appropriate incentive, in certain circumstances, helps airlines commit to new air service to satisfy any new route passengers' more satisfactory flying needs.

Similarly, the strategy steps follow: benchmark air services, identify deficiencies, identify new route opportunities, identify potential air service providers, assess viability of potential air services and prioritize route opportunities and target carriers.

Any airlines may find any information concerns new route business cases to decide their countries flying new routes choice , such as: catchment area profile: demographics, economy, tourist etc. information, airport profile : traffic and facilities information market profile; market sizes , top city pairs, traffic leakage etc. information, suggested service : frequency , schedule, airport routing information, route analysis: market share, load factor, stimulation potential, self-diversion etc. information, any airlines' past flying routes strategic considerations etc. information in order to predict and evaluate whether how many further passenger number is flying that they accept to choose the new flying routes travelling needs.

Hence, how to design to impact either the supply or demand for any new flight routes that is only important because of the country has less number of passengers accept to choose the new flying route to fly. Then, the new flying route does not needed to be design to supply to the country's travelling passengers because their acceptance to this new flying route ends are very less. However, the demand level is low new flying route needs to satisfy these three qualifying services criteria, such as: Are new routes only? Increase on existing routes? Does it work service rent incentives? Will the new flying route be satisfied to air service to the airline passengers and airport waiting passengers, e.g. strategically important? Marginally (unprofitable) self-sustaining in the short term? New flying routes only? Increase an existing routes? Service rent incentives?

How can airports afford aggressive airline incentive / fee discounts and still fund route development marketing in a difficult economy? I recommend that the solution method may include new flying route design and developing and maximizing non-aeronautical revenue streams both, such as retail and duty free, food and beverage, parking , loyalty and premium programs and land development to airport building. Marketing funding strategy may be an ineffective incentive for travelling destinations. However, it may not differentiate a market, as route marketing incentives are used by over 80% of communities in the U.S. marketing incentives can be: Unilateral airport pays 100% or cooperative airlines matches some portion, funding amounts are often tied on the capacity of inbound seats to be available on the new flight (flying) route. By calculating the economic impact of new visitors (spend at the destination), a destination can calculate the return on investment in cooperative new flight (flying) route market.

On conclusion, air connectivity is one important factor to influence any country's travelling passengers to the airline's service quality or service level in order to achieve new flying (flight) route design , reducing inflight transfer another airplane waiting time in airport, or marketing development in success. So, any airlines can not neglect this air connectivity will influence their passengers' service quality. Hence, air connectivity factor is also very important to influence any travelling passengers' service satisfactory level.

How to measure and rise airline
service quality

How are airline performing ? Nowadays, the rise of the low cost airlines' competition is serious, due to airlines hope to rise themselves attractions to influence passengers to choose to use their travelling services. So, different airlines have spend long time to build their unique person-to-person passenger services, which passengers use of different airlines, e.g. digital electronic air tickets purchase method. Any airlines hope to make each journey personalized to the individual will gain market share and improve its service quality to be more unique in order to reach the efforts of airlines to build high levels of customer service appears to have been generally noticed by passengers, when they choose to buy the airline's digital electronic ticket or paper air ticket to use its flying service.

Hence, improvement their digital e-ticket purchase experience and communications factor, for example, if any passengers can enter the airline's air ticket purchase website to buy electronic ticket to pre-book seats in the short time rapidly as well as there are enough seats number to supply to them to pre-book. So, they do not need to worry about without any seats to supply to them to catch the airline's flight to fly to anywhere in any time available conveniently. So, it seems that there is plenty of space for airlines to grow and improve their digital experience and communication method to let any passengers to feel, if the airline hopes to let its passengers to feel that it has unique service to compare others airlines.

The aviation industry plays a major role in the aspect of work and leisure to passengers around the global. So, nowadays passengers' demands to any airlines' service quality had been raised. Hence, any airline service industry messengers are under pressure to prove their services are customers oriented service improvement of performance that guarantees competitive advantages to the global travelling marketplace. So, it also implies that any airlines' services performance will be influenced to cause many passengers feel more poor and let passengers dissatisfy the airline's service performance. The, the airline will possible lose many passengers, due to passengers have many airlines choices, they can find any airlines to replace which any one airline to buy air ticket from internet at home immediately.

However, airlines' comfortable seats arrangement service provision feeling factor is still important in preferable to compare other factors, because passengers must need to sit any seats in any air planes. So, whether the air plane can provide new comfortable seats to let passengers to feel this factor is still the most important factor to influence any passengers to choose to the airline's air plane to catch. For example, service comfortability is how passengers observed the quality of service offered them by the airline's cleanliness, quiet zone, shops, restaurants and business pavilion in functioning like staffs, information desk, and in flight announcement are included as tangible features by the passengers (Geraldine et a.,2013). All of these factors are needed often to measure whether their service performances are satisfactory to themselves passengers service needs.

Moreover, the other factors may include service affordability , it can be regarded as given passenger the opportunity to select from inclusive air ticket prices made available to the different group of passengers by the airlines, as a gesture of goodwill , to establish and reinforce customer loyalty and repeat purchases essential for the airline continuity as well as service reliability. it is the probability that airline will carry out its expected function satisfactory as stated in the flight schedule. Hence, there is a strong link between different airlines' service quality variables, airline image and repeat patronage from the passengers.

Service quality is a measure of how well the service level delivered matches passengers expectations to measure service quality based on input from focus groups. It consists of five factors (tangibles, reliability, responsiveness, assurance and empathy). All of these factors will be identifies that how the airline service quality can be satisfactory to its passengers ' psychological and emotion enjoyable service needs.

Any one of these any five service factors will be important to influence the airline's passengers service feeling level to the airline. It means that the passenger will have more chance to choose the airline's service again (repeating purchase its air ticket). Hence, any airlines can not neglect any one of service feeling to its passengers. It needs often to enquire questionnaires to evaluate whether its these five aspects of service quality , if it discovered any of these five aspects of service level is poor, e.g. 5 scale is the best service performance level, then it can attempt to find its error whether which aspects, it needs to very need to reach the 5 scale , the best service performance level when many passengers feel, e.g. enquiring 100 passengers who give 5 scale to reliability service aspect, before reliability service aspect has less than 50% passengers from 100 passengers who feel the airlines concerns this reliable service level aspect questions to be the best. It is one kind of measurement service quality method to any airlines.

Other service performance evaluation factor is satisfaction in the job to every airline front service or ground service staffs to the airline. Job satisfaction describes how content an employee is with his or her job. It is how the employee responses to a job. It can be considered as a part of life satisfaction to one organization, when the employee is working in the organization. Hence, if one airline front service as ground service staff who can feel more job satisfaction to compare his/her prior airline employer. Then, he/she won't be easy to change his/her present airline employer.

However, some factors can influence job satisfaction are pay and benefit, fair performance appraisal, career and promotional opportunities, proper reward and recognition, work-family life balance, the job itself, proper working conditions, leadership chance, autonomy in work.

Job satisfaction can also involve complex number of variables, circumstances, opinions and behavioral tendencies and a variety of work related outcomes, such as commitment, involvement, motivation, satisfaction, attendance. Hence, any airlines also need to concern how let their employees feel job satisfaction issue in order to avoid their leaving turnover number increases, due to job satisfaction and dissatisfaction depend on the expectations what the job supplies for an employee not the nature of the job.

Finally, instead of concerning employees job satisfaction issue, any airlines also need to concern passengers satisfaction issue because it will have any passengers will choose the airline, if it can bring more service satisfaction to let them to feel , then they will become repeat passengers to the airline.

What kinds of factors passengers were looking for and what were the reasons of choosing a specific airline? When one airline often is complained from its passengers. It will have more mistakes to let them to feel or dissatisfy its service. Hence the airlines needs to find which are its mistakes and improve in order to satisfy its passengers' expectations, e.g. finding what are the mistakes to the airlines' serious concern regarding passenger complaints and complaint satisfaction in order to make the airline more likely to meet its passengers' expectation in case of a problem. Hence, any airlines need to concern how to improve its employees' satisfactory service as well as its passengers' satisfactory service both issues as well as how to measure their service quality whether is enough to achieve general service acceptable performance to its passengers.

Reference

A bed, S. Y. A.O. Ba-Fail and S.M. Jasimuddin (2001), " An economatic analysis of international air travel demand in Saudi Arabia". Journal of air transport managmement, vol. 7, pp.143-148.

Bamber, L., & Dale, B.G. Lean production : a study of application in a traditoinal manufacturing environment. Production planning & control, 11 (3), 291-298, 2000.

Dobruszkes, F.M. Lennert and G. Van Hamme (2011). " An analysis of the determinants of air traffic volume for European metropolitan area". Journal of transport geographyy, vol. 19/4/pp.755-762.

Gealdine, O., & David , U.C. (2013). effects of airline service quality on airline image and passengers' loyalty:

Findings from Arill Air Nigeria passengers, Journal of hospitality and management tourism, 4(2), 19-28. doi: http://dx.doi: 10.5897/HMT 2013, 0089.

Glass, R., Seifermann, S., & Metternich, J. The spread of lean production in the assembly, Process and maching industry. Procedia CIRP, 55, 278-283, 2016.

Guller, M. & Guller, M. (2003) From Airport to airport city. Editional Gustavo , Gili, Barcel on a.Intervistas Consulting Inc.

Massachusetts Institute Of Technology (MIT), Lean Aerospace Initiative, Available: www.lean.mit.edu, 2005.